What experts say about this book

Dr. Weinstein has translated the ACT essay instruction she regularly gives to her students into a methodical, easy-to-use guide for any student wishing to master the ACT essay. This workbook is full of realistic ACT-style essay prompts with the classic three perspectives that take the student from clear examples to completed essays. Later in the workbook are prompts that require more and more input from the student; a student can employ this step-by-step approach for independent study or with the help of a professional.

I know that I'll be using this book from now on.

– **Kate Dalby, President, Inspiring Test Preparation, Inc.**

I love the way Winning Strategies for ACT Writing Essays deconstructs the test. With the guide's detailed focus on everything from analyzing the prompt and creating a topic sentence to presenting a counter argument, students can really hone in on the specific skills they need to develop. I wish all prep books were as easy to follow! The skills reinforced in this book will not only improve students' scores but also make them stronger writers, which will have a lifelong impact.

– **Reena Kamins, Independent Educational Consultant, College, Career & Life**

Reading Aimee Weinstein's *Winning Strategies for ACT Essay Writing* is like having a friendly and knowledgeable teacher sitting across the table talking just to you. Such comfortable teaching is what Aimee has always done in her professional career, and now she does it with her book on how to write for the ACT. Aimee's approach is to isolate the most important points of writing well, but her own writing style is the magic that makes the instruction natural and easy to follow. Her explanations are clear, well-organized, and phrased in a lively manner that teens will appreciate. Particularly helpful are the 15 example essays with Aimee's markings and comments. The book's information will assist all types of learners as the graphic charts and marked essays are effectively presented. *Winning Strategies for ACT Essay Writing* will be welcomed by both students and tutors — as well as worried parents not knowing how to help their children with the ACT.

– **Cathy Colglazier, English Chair at McLean and TJHSST**

What experts say about this book!

As a SAT & ACT strategist, I am always excited to explore new channels or content or learning & came across this book that deconstructs Essay section for the ACT.

This book has wide range of essays (with solutions) that are relevant to ACT exam. Author has decoded the ACT Essay in a very systematic & analytical approach meanwhile keeping it simple. Few initial pages only win you over with brief & crisp description of essay part in ACT. The versatile examples & highly organized outline helps students who are poor/average essay writer (including yours' truly) to get grasp of section easily. Author provides you with set templates to learn/follow which should fit almost all topics & bisects the content for every paragraph beautifully. Marked essays makes learning a joy where one can deep dive into the context, elevating thought process & creating a right structure.

This book is easy to understand, simple to follow & I would say it's a must have for beginners struggling to ace ACT Essay.

– Chinu Vasudeva, Founder & Mentor, Doyen-Ed

Don't take the ACT without first reading Dr. Weinstein's Winning Strategies for ACT Essay Writing! This books takes you through every step of the essay writing process, including how to analyze the question, select the best position, manage your time with precision, and finish the test with a fantastic score. The 15 sample prompts are expertly crafted and will provide all the practice you need, whether you're studying on your own or working with a tutor.

– Heather Krey, Director, Test Prep for Success

VIBRANT
PUBLISHERS

WINNING STRATEGIES FOR

ACT®

ESSAY WRITING:

WITH 15 SAMPLE PROMPTS

2022

Analyze each prompt

Use the allotted
time effectively

Plan the essay carefully

Self Evaluate
sample essays

Increase your confidence

Third Edition

DR. AIMEE WEINSTEIN

Winning Strategies For ACT® Essay Writing: With 15 Sample Prompts
Third Edition

Paperback ISBN-10: 1-63651-049-3
Paperback ISBN-13: 978-1-63651-049-1

E-book ISBN-10: 1-63651-050-7
E-book ISBN-13: 978-1-63651-050-7
Library of Congress Control Number: 2019948862

This publication is designed to provide accurate and authoritative information in regard to the subject matter covered. The Author has made every effort in the preparation of this book to ensure the accuracy of the information. However, information in this book is sold without warranty either expressed or implied. The Author or the Publisher will not be liable for any damages caused or alleged to be caused either directly or indirectly by this book.

Vibrant Publishers books are available at special quantity discount for sales promotions, or for use in corporate training programs. For more information please write to **bulkorders@vibrantpublishers.com**

Please email feedback / corrections (technical, grammatical or spelling) to **spellerrors@vibrantpublishers.com**

For general inquires please write to **reachus@vibrantpublishers.com**

To access the complete catalogue of Vibrant Publishers, visit **www.vibrantpublishers.com**

*ACT is a registered trademark of ACT, Inc. which neither sponsors nor endorses this product.

Table of Contents

Dear Student/Parent/Tutor –

Thank you for purchasing **Winning Strategies For ACT Essay Writing: With 15 Sample Prompts.** We are committed to publishing books that are content-rich, concise and approachable enabling more students to read and make the fullest use of them. We hope this book provides the most enriching learning experience as you prepare for your **ACT** exam.

Should you have any questions or suggestions, feel free to email us at **reachus@vibrantpublishers.com**

Thanks again for your purchase. Good luck for your ACT!

– Vibrant Publishers Team

ACT/SAT Books in Test Prep Series

Math Practice Tests for the ACT
ISBN: 978-1-63651-085-9

SAT Math Practice Questions
ISBN: 978-1-63651-094-1

Practice Tests For The SAT
ISBN: 978-1-63651-087-3

For the most updated list of books visit
www.vibrantpublishers.com

About the author

Dr. Aimee Weinstein is a writer and professor whose passion is coaching students on how to write effective essays for college applications as well as the ACT and SAT. She works full-time at George Mason University in Fairfax, Virginia as a Term Assistant Professor of Humanities and Graduate Pathway Advisor with INTO Mason. Dr. Weinstein works with the INTO Mason Mentoring Committee and is part of the Mason Faculty Learning Community on the Study of Teaching and Learning. She received her doctorate from the Department of Higher Education at George Mason University where she focused on teaching writing to second language learners via a hybrid classroom. Dr. Weinstein lived for more than ten years in Tokyo, Japan where she taught writing at Temple University, Japan. She has held positions at The George Washington University and Prince George's Community College (MD), teaching classes in various levels and genres of writing. Her previous publications include several food and travel articles in English-language magazines in Japan. Dr. Weinstein currently lives in McLean, Virginia.

Acknowledgements

Thank you to Ethan Dixon, writer extraordinaire, who helped with the sample essays in this book. Thanks also to intern Sakshi Ashar, who has helped us with many of the ideas that have shaped this book into its structure of success. And lastly, thank you to my loving and tolerant family, including my two kids, who have been through the ACT process and have been the guinea pigs of many prompts, as well as my darling husband, Marc, who creates the environment in which I can write. I am grateful beyond measure.

This page is intentionally left blank.

I

About the ACT Essay

Introduction

The ACT itself was developed in the mid-twentieth century as an alternative to the SAT. It is comprised of four main sections, English, Math, Reading and Scientific Reasoning. Traditionally it is thought of as measuring more of what students know, rather than how they use what they know, but as time has gone on, the focus on reasoning has increased in importance. Most colleges do not prefer one test to the other, but still most often require students to submit scores from one or the other. Some schools are becoming "test optional" so that the tests are not required, but most students are still taking the tests just in case one of their top choice universities require them. The test is offered at testing centers around the US and abroad upwards of seven times a year. While still important, the essay section of the ACT is indeed optional – students can take the test with or without the essay. It is up to the individual schools to which the student is applying whether or not the essay score is required for a complete application to that institution.

Welcome to the ACT Essay! Once you master the method of approaching the prompt, you might even have a bit of fun with the process. The essay is based on not only formulating an opinion on a given topic, but also understanding and addressing various sides to an argument. The people who score the test will look for your ability to think through a problem, understand multiple perspectives on the problem with deep nuance and then to explain your approach to the issue while also defending why your idea is the best one among the multiple perspectives.

The essay is an optional section of the ACT and is taken AFTER the 3 hours of testing has taken place. Students will have 40 minutes to read the prompt, analyze the given perspectives, formulate a response and then write. While the ACT itself is computer-based, the essay is hand-written.

Schools have a choice whether or not to require that applicants for admission sit for the essay in addition to the test. There is not one right or wrong way; some schools see the essay as valuable while others do not. Those schools that tend to look at the essay are looking to assess thinking process as much as the ability to put sentences together in a coherent format. When making decisions on whether or not to sit for the ACT essay, it is good to have an idea of which schools you will be applying to, so you know if you have to take the essay section. If you do not yet have a list of schools, then it behooves you to sit for the essay section because if just one of your desired schools requires it and you have not yet taken it, then you will have to take the entire ACT over again to engage with the essay. You cannot just sit for the essay without taking the full exam.

When approaching this task, we strongly recommend that you PLAN your work before you

write. A general guideline is to spend 10 minutes reading the prompt and planning what you will write (along with your Pro-Con chart deconstructing the argument – see below) and then 30 minutes actually writing. Ideally you would spend 25 minutes writing and 5 minutes checking over your work, but most students cannot manage their time that closely. Do give it a try though!

About the Prompt

The ACT essay prompt is generally a paragraph about some sort of social issue. It can range from computers taking over jobs, to the pros and cons of owning a pet. The essay is designed for students to show how they think through an issue and explain how they arrived at their ideas. While issues generally have two sides to them – pro and con, the ACT essay requires more nuance than that.

The prompt offers three perspectives, two of which are normally very closely related to each other. The prompt and the perspectives could be addressing a very small part of a larger issue or it could be combining issues in creative ways. For example, an essay might not be just asking students to take a side on whether it's good to recycle or not, but rather, might require students to think about whether or not it is economically feasible to recycle in most cities. The perspectives will offer ideas on the sides of an issue, which is great when an issue arises that a student has not considered before, but then the student still has to arrive at his or her own approach to the problem. Often, it's easiest to agree with one of the perspectives and to refute the other, but sometimes there's a way to combine the perspectives into a new, coherent argument to address the problem.

Formulating an Opinion

There are many ways to formulate an opinion, and as a student, you are just learning to think through problems to arrive at the best idea possible for you personally. The graders of the ACT essay do not grade you on the validity of your opinion, rather your ability to describe it, provide details about it and defend it. When approaching this essay task, you have a limited time to think through the problem, outline the essay, and then write it, so you need to practice creating opinions. Read newspaper articles and see what you think; examine your own ideas; talk to friends and family members about issues; do anything you can to practice deciding what you think and coming down on one side of an argument. Luckily the way the prompts are written with three perspectives included, you will be able to choose one to defend most fully while still addressing the others (without using the words "in perspective one.. in perspective two…!!) so

ACT Essay

you can make a choice right there during the test. Defend the perspective that most fully aligns with your point of view because you will be more successful if you believe in what you're writing.

Approaching the Perspectives/Planning the essay

You might be asking, if there are two sides to any issue, then why does the ACT essay present three perspectives? Good question. One answer is that it helps students to see the nuances and thoughts surrounding the issue. Another answer is that the three perspectives help students formulate some sort of middle-ground opinion. But really what students must do first, before anything else, is understand what the prompt is really asking so they can **Deconstruct the Argument.**

The first step in approaching the prompt is to figure out what the prompt is really asking. For example, if the example prompt gives a whole paragraph on the economics of recycling, students should think about the intersection of money and environmentalism, and no matter what the THREE perspectives look like, they should find the simple, two sides of the issue before doing anything else.

Deconstruct the Argument – figure out what the prompt is really asking. So, the sides of the issue might look like this:

Pros: recycling cans and bottles in a city of a million people makes sound economic sense due to the reduction of greenhouse gases and the creation of a cleaner city.

Cons: recycling cans and bottles costs a city more money in waste removal and storage than the savings it engenders.

I would urge students to actually make a Pro-Con chart on their papers before they start writing. Like this:

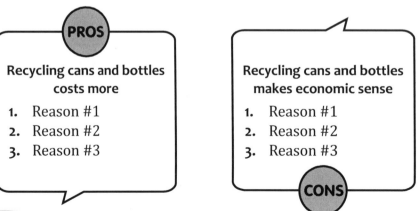

PROS

Recycling cans and bottles costs more

1. Reason #1
2. Reason #2
3. Reason #3

Recycling cans and bottles makes economic sense

1. Reason #1
2. Reason #2
3. Reason #3

CONS

Writing Paragraphs

The "reasons" in the Pro-Con chart above then morph into your paragraphs. A sample outline might look like this:

Paragraph 1: *Introduction, including thesis statement taking one of the sides*
Paragraph 2: *Your side of the argument including one of the reasons and examples*
Paragraph 3: *Another reason your side of the argument is correct, including examples*
Paragraph 4: *The other side of the argument – counter argument including several examples*
Paragraph 5: *The other side of the argument – counter argument including several examples*

Best practice Tip: Before you begin writing, make the Pro-Con chart where you deconstruct the argument, then write your thesis statement. If you have time, jot down a few words of what will go into each paragraph. THEN begin writing. The thinking and planning might take a full ten minutes of your forty minutes, but that is okay because putting in that effort up front will ensure that the other thirty minutes will be well-used.

Scoring

The ACT essay is scored out of 12 points. The ACT specially trains graders and each essay is graded by two people. Each one gives a score of 1-6 in four categories: ideas and analysis, development and support, organization, and language use. There is a total score of 12 possible points for each category. These category scores are then averaged into a total score out of 12.

The graders take care when scoring the essays to ensure that their categories are fully met. In the category of language usage, the graders expect good grammar, strong vocabulary and varied sentences. The ideas and analysis mostly measures a student's ability to approach the prompt and formulate the opinion. Success in the category of organization depends on students creating strong, unified paragraphs that focus on one point – analyzing and thinking through it fully before moving on to the next paragraph and the next idea. Most often students have the most trouble with the development and support category because in order to be successful, students must truly drill down into the topic and provide details as to why their point of view is valid. The details of the explanations are crucial to the success of the paragraphs – be as specific as possible with explanations and specifics.

For more details, please see the official ACT essay scoring rubric which is included as under:

(**Credit:** *https://www.act.org/content/dam/act/unsecured/documents/Writing-Test-Scoring-Rubric.pdf*)

	Ideas and Analysis	Development and Support	Organization	Language Use
Score 6: **Responses at this scorepoint demonstrate effective skill in writing an argumentative essay.**	The writer generates an argument that critically engages with multiple perspectives on the given issue. The argument's thesis reflects nuance and precision in thought and purpose. The argument establishes and employs an insightful context for analysis of the issue and its perspectives. The analysis examines implications, complexities and tensions, and/or underlying values and assumptions.	Development of ideas and support for claims deepen insight and broaden context. An integrated line of skillful reasoning and illustration effectively bolster ideas and conveys the significance of the argument. Qualifications and complications enrich and bolster ideas and analysis.	The response exhibits a skillful organizational strategy. The response is unified by a controlling idea or purpose, and a logical progression of ideas increases the effectiveness of the writer's argument. Transitions between and within paragraphs strengthen the relationships among ideas.	The use of language enhances the argument. Word choice is skillful and precise. Sentence structures are consistent, varied, and clear. Stylistic and register choices, including voice and tone, are strategic and effective. While a few minor errors in grammar, usage, and mechanics may be present, they do not impede understanding
Score 5: **Responses at this scorepoint demonstrate well-developed skill in writing an argumentative essay.**	The writer generates an argument that productively engages with multiple perspectives on the given issue. The argument's thesis reflects precision in thought and purpose. The argument establishes and employs a thoughtful context for analysis of the issue and its perspectives. The analysis addresses implications, complexities and tensions, and/or underlying values and assumptions.	Development of ideas and support for claims deepen understanding. A mostly integrated line of purposeful reasoning and illustration capably conveys the significance of the argument. Qualifications and complications enrich ideas and analysis.	The response exhibits a productive organizational strategy. The response is mostly unified by a controlling idea or purpose, and a logical sequencing of ideas contributes to the effectiveness of the argument. Transitions between and within paragraphs consistently clarify the relationships among ideas.	The use of language works in service of the argument. Word choice is precise. Sentence structures are clear and varied often. Stylistic and register choices, including voice and tone, are purposeful and productive. While minor errors in grammar, usage, and mechanics may be present, they do not impede understanding.

Credit: https://www.act.org/content/dam/act/unsecured/documents/Writing-Test-Scoring-Rubric.pdf

(continued)

ACT Essay

	Ideas and Analysis	Development and Support	Organization	Language Use
Score 4: **Responses at this scorepoint demonstrate adequate skill in writing an argumentative essay.**	The writer generates an argument that engages with multiple perspectives on the given issue. The argument's thesis reflects clarity in thought and purpose. The argument establishes and employs a relevant context for analysis of the issue and its perspectives. The analysis recognizes implications, complexities and tensions, and/or underlying values and assumptions.	Development of ideas and support for claims clarify meaning and purpose. Lines of clear reasoning and illustration adequately convey the significance of the argument. Qualifications and complications extend ideas and analysis.	The response exhibits a clear organizational strategy. The overall shape of the response reflects an emergent controlling idea or purpose. Ideas are logically grouped and sequenced. Transitions between and within paragraphs clarify the relationships among ideas.	The use of language conveys the argument with clarity. Word choice is adequate and sometimes precise. Sentence structures are clear and demonstrate some variety. Stylistic and register choices, including voice and tone, are appropriate for the rhetorical purpose. While errors in grammar, usage, and mechanics are present, they rarely impede understanding.
Score 3: **Responses at this scorepoint demonstrate some developing skill in writing an argumentative essay.**	The writer generates an argument that responds to multiple perspectives on the given issue. The argument's thesis reflects some clarity in thought and purpose. The argument establishes a limited or tangential context for analysis of the issue and its perspectives. Analysis is simplistic or somewhat unclear.	Development of ideas and support for claims are mostly relevant but are overly general or simplistic. Reasoning and illustration largely clarify the argument but may be somewhat repetitious or imprecise.	The response exhibits a basic organizational structure. The response largely coheres, with most ideas logically grouped. Transitions between and within paragraphs sometimes clarify the relationships among ideas.	The use of language is basic and only somewhat clear. Word choice is general and occasionally imprecise. Sentence structures are usually clear but show little variety. Stylistic and register choices, including voice and tone, are not always appropriate for the rhetorical purpose. Distracting errors in grammar, usage, and mechanics may be present, but they generally do not impede understanding

Credit: https://www.act.org/content/dam/act/unsecured/documents/Writing-Test-Scoring-Rubric.pdf

(continued)

ACT Essay

	Ideas and Analysis	Development and Support	Organization	Language Use
Score 2: **Responses at this scorepoint demonstrate weak or inconsistent skill in writing an argumentative essay.**	The writer generates an argument that weakly responds to multiple perspectives on the given issue. The argument's thesis, if evident, reflects little clarity in thought and purpose. Attempts at analysis are incomplete, largely irrelevant, or consist primarily of restatement of the issue and its perspectives.	Development of ideas and support for claims are weak, confused, or disjointed. Reasoning and illustration are inadequate, illogical, or circular, and fail to fully clarify the argument.	The response exhibits a rudimentary organizational structure. Grouping of ideas is inconsistent and often unclear. Transitions between and within paragraphs are misleading or poorly formed.	The use of language is inconsistent and often unclear. Word choice is rudimentary and frequently imprecise. Sentence structures are sometimes unclear. Stylistic and register choices, including voice and tone, are inconsistent and are not always appropriate for the rhetorical purpose. Distracting errors in grammar, usage, and mechanics are present, and they sometimes impede understanding.
Score 1: **Responses at this scorepoint demonstrate little or no skill in writing an argumentative essay.**	The writer fails to generate an argument that responds intelligibly to the task. The writer's intentions are difficult to discern. Attempts at analysis are unclear or irrelevant.	Ideas lack development and claims lack support. Reasoning and illustration are unclear, incoherent, or largely absent.	The response does not exhibit an organizational structure. There is little grouping of ideas. When present, transitional devices fail to connect ideas.	The use of language fails to demonstrate skill in responding to the task. Word choice is imprecise and often difficult to comprehend. Sentence structures are often unclear. Stylistic and register choices are difficult to identify. Errors in grammar, usage, and mechanics are pervasive and often impede understanding.

Credit: https://www.act.org/content/dam/act/unsecured/documents/Writing-Test-Scoring-Rubric.pdf

ACT Essay

Ten Best Practices for success

Thesis	**1**	Your thesis is the road map to the essay – be sure it is clear and specific
Sentence Construction	**2**	Be sure to use strong, clear verbs, not passive constructions
Handwriting	**3**	Use your very best penmanship
Analysis	**4**	Analyze all points fully – give an example that proves the point and then show how and why it proves your point.
Counter-Argument	**5**	Be sure to include a counter-argument paragraph so the graders know that you can think through the nuance of an issue
Conclusion	**6**	Have a strong conclusion even if it looks very similar to the introduction
Topic Sentence	**7**	Use clear, specific topic sentences to lay out your claim at the top of each paragraph
Grammar	**8**	Use good grammar and punctuation and other writing conventions
Flow of Thoughts	**9**	Transition smoothly between paragraphs
Support	**10**	Be creative yet logical in your proof and argumentation. Convince your readers that your perspective is the only valid one.

ACT Essay

How to use this guide

This ACT essay guide can be used by both individual students and tutors with their students. After you read through this introduction, you will see that we have written fifteen prompts and have them solved. For the first two prompts, we have suggestions for writing with the prompts on the same pages. These suggestions are meant to help students learn to not only write the main points of the essay, but to also incorporate the essential details necessary to explain those points and help the reader fully understand the writer's intentions. You should study these details and then use the ideas for every essay going forward.

For the following prompts we put more and more information about the approaches to the prompts in the Solutions section at the end of the book instead of right with the prompts themselves so students have a chance to think through their responses before seeing the answers laid out right in front of them. This format will give you a way to practice writing your topic sentences and details so you can become proficient at it by the time you work on the 15th prompt.

The goal of this book is to help students learn to solve the problems – think through the essay responses – by themselves, but if they need the help, it is available in the Solutions section. There is an explanation of the best way to approach and "solve" the prompts – and write the essay – for fifteen prompts. The authors have made significant suggestions on the best way to go about thinking through the problems and we hope by the time the students have gone through all fifteen prompts that they will see the patterns and requirements of the essay for themselves so that the method can be easily translated to any prompt the student receives on the actual test.

Also, for fifteen prompts we have included sample essays in response to those prompts. These sample essays are our best efforts and putting the thoughts into practice. Hopefully you will be able to study them and learn what we feel is the best way to put the words around the important ideas you must explain.

One note about timing for the essay section of the ACT: you have 40 minutes total to complete it. You will want to spend at least 5-10 minutes planning your essay – thinking through and writing your deconstruction of the prompt, and your thesis. Then you should write your topic sentences in response to those details. THEN you can begin your essay with about 30 minutes to go. If all goes well, you can spare the last two minutes to proofread a little bit before finishing. This book has timing notes at the start so you can see the suggested timing and then note your actual timing as you practice.

For the e-edition of this book, we have designed Planning sheets and Answer sheets that may be printed and used by students to work through their approach to each essay prompt and to finally write the essay. They are available for download from the product page of this book on *www.vibrantpublishers.com*.

Lastly, we have included five more prompts that do not have explanations or sample essays so that the students can test what they have learned throughout the book. Good luck and enjoy the process!

ESSAY 1

Advertising in Schools

Analysis	Solved
Deconstruct	Solved
Outline	Solved
Sample Essay	Solved

	Reading time	Planning time	Writing time
Recommended	5 mins	5 mins	30 mins
Actual	_____	_____	_____

Advertising in Schools

Many public high schools in the U.S. are looking to increase funds for special programs, sporting events and other activities. One solution some school districts have supported is allowing companies to place advertisements around the campus. Some schools allow local businesses to place banners along the fences of the football fields. Some academic institutions might have advertising boards in the front hallway of the school buildings or even advertisements running along the side of the school or even announcements on strategically placed screens throughout the buildings. Regardless of where the ads are placed, some people feel that students should not be seeing outside advertising during their school day. The local businesses might be advertising products or services that parents do not support or do not want their children exposed to. However, if the students need a product or service that has been advertised in the school, they would be more likely to support a company that supports their school. If the underlying purpose of the advertisements is to generate revenue for the school, what is the real harm in allowing the businesses to promote their products?

Read and carefully consider these perspectives. Each suggests a particular way of thinking about including advertisements in school environments.

Perspective One	**Perspective Two**	**Perspective Three**
Advertising does not belong in schools. It distracts students from learning, and they might be exposed to products or services their parents would not support. If the school district cannot rely on government funding or parent contributions, then any potential new program should be cut.	School districts have a right to obtain funding wherever they can so they should vet businesses based on their student population and accept funding from them in order to keep specialized programs moving forward and even implement new programs.	School districts should poll their parent populations and decide whether or not raising funds via advertising is a good idea. If the parents decide against such measures, then it would be up to those parents to secure funding for specialized programs.

ESSAY 1

Essay Task

Write a unified, coherent essay about advertising in schools. In your essay, be sure to:

- Clearly state your own perspective on the issue and analyze the relationship between your perspective and at least one other perspective
- Develop and support your ideas with reasoning and examples
- Organize your ideas clearly and logically
- Communicate your ideas effectively in standard written English

Your perspective may be in full agreement with any of those given, in partial agreement or completely different.

ANALYSIS OF THE PROMPT

What is this prompt really asking?

What really matters here is whether or not the student is seeing advertisements in school, regardless of whether it is on the football field or in the middle of the school hallway. The thing to keep in mind is the nuance of the perspectives. While the prompt is straightforward, it is also asking WHO should be the decision-maker in this instance.

Should parents have a say in what their children see daily?
Does an advertisement in a high school from a local business promote a sense of community?

These are the side issues to consider when creating your Pro-Con chart to deconstruct the argument.

ESSAY 1

DECONSTRUCT THE ARGUMENT

PROS

Schools Can Show Advertisements.

1. The money schools raise from ads is crucial to funding programs and events.

2. The local businesses that support the schools create community morale.

3. If students need a product or service advertised in school, then they can support businesses that support their school.

Schools Should Not Have Ads.

1. The ads might be for products or services that are not good/healthy for students.

2. The ads might be for products or services the parents do not support.

3. The ad revenue might go to programs or events the school does not actually need.

CONS

From here, you should write a *thesis statement* that looks something like this:

"Allowing local businesses to advertise their products and services in schools is a good way to generate revenue for the school but parents should have a say in deciding precisely which companies get to market to their children."

OUTLINE

Introduction and thesis statement

Tip: Hook with a comment about football or watching something on a screen in a school.

Paragraph 1

Topic sentence

The money schools raise from ads is crucial to funding programs and events.

Tip: Schools with underprivileged populations need extra funding and this is one way to help get it – mention specific clubs like the Model U.N. club that wants to travel or badly needed new band uniforms.

Paragraph 2

Topic sentence

If students need a product or service advertised in school then they could support businesses that support their school.

Tip: Be as specific as possible! Perhaps the local hardware store advertises in the school so if a parent needs something, they will frequent that particular shop that supports the school.

Paragraph 3

Counter argument topic sentence

While advertising in schools generates revenue, it can also promote products that parents are not comfortable exposing their children to, so parents of students in the school should vote on whether the product is appropriate or not.

Tip: Continue to be specific – some parents do not want their children to see ads for sugary sodas, but the school receives money from drink companies, so they place the ads. The money is too good to turn down, but parents might be upset.

Paragraph 4

ESSAY 1

Paragraph 5

Conclusion and re-statement of thesis

Tip: Be sure to use different wording for the thesis statement and conclude strongly with your ideas for the topic or future directions.

This essay can easily be written from either perspective or using different examples. The key here is to focus on the argument you have deconstructed so you can stay focused on one idea per paragraph and be organized. Each paragraph should have one to two examples and each example should be analyzed to connect it to the topic sentence or even the thesis statement before transitioning to the next paragraph.

ESSAY 1

SAMPLE ESSAY

Advertising in Schools

Sometimes people drive past high schools and notice big banners hanging from the fences surrounding the school. Some of them promote the school and various clubs and athletic events, but some of them are advertisements for businesses. The schools raise money by allowing certain ads not only facing the outside of the school, but also inside where students are intimately exposed to their messages. Allowing local businesses to advertise their products and services in schools is a good way to generate revenue for the school but parents should have a say in deciding precisely which companies get to market to their children."

Introduction and thesis statement

The money schools raise from ads is crucial to funding programs and events. Even the wealthiest school districts in the U.S. could use more funding; everyone always wants to do more and have more. They key is schools in underprivileged areas of the country; in those places the revenue raised by allowing ads in school allows the band to have new uniforms, the Model U.N. club to travel to a conference and maybe even for the bleachers on the football field to be repaired. These are things that the Federal and State money does not fund because they are often labeled as "extras" that the school doesn't need per se but adds to the atmosphere of the community. If the school did not use advertising revenue for these extras, then the parents might have to give money to the school, which is often not an option in already tight family budgets. Advertising revenue is important to the school for the little extras that make a school into a community.

Supporting Paragraph: Example 1

The community aspect plays into the particular businesses that are allowed to advertise in the schools because often they are local businesses. If students need a product or service advertised in school, then they could support businesses that support their school. In the local town where we live, a small, family-owned hardware shop pays to have a banner on the football field as well as a small ad in the school newspaper. Students become intimately familiar with the name of the store and if the student or their parents need something hardware related, they are more likely to stop at the small store rather than find a big-box shop that does not advertise in their school and take part in the community.

Supporting Paragraph: More examples

ESSAY 1

Counter Argument with examples

On the flip side, while advertising in schools generates revenue, it can also promote products that parents are not comfortable exposing their children to, so parents of students in the school should at least have input on whether the product is appropriate or not. Some schools allow advertisements for soda or other sugary products that parents do not want their children to see, so perhaps parents could have some sort of vote on what constitutes appropriate content. There will always be disagreement and some things are subject to taste, but if everyone keeps in mind the goal of generating revenue for the students, then it should be fine for parents to comment on what is advertised and where in the school.

Conclusion

Allowing businesses, particularly local ones, to advertise in schools has the potential to raise revenue to fund crucial programs as well as create a sense of community within the school. If parents are allowed to comment on the content their children see daily then raising revenue from outside the school and government should be a great way to support our students.

ESSAY 1

ESSAY 2

Politics and Star Power

Analysis	**Solved**
Deconstruct	**Solved**
Outline	**Solved**
Sample Essay	**Solved**

	Reading time	Planning time	Writing time
Recommended	5 mins	5 mins	30 mins
Actual	_____	_____	_____

Politics and Star Power

In today's day and age information and opinions are available on any topic at the click of a button. People who have the public's attention for any reason, including stars of the stage and screen, can express their opinions on any topic via various types of media and thus influence political opinions of the audience who reveres them. Actors tweet their political viewpoints; they give speeches at political conventions; and they appear at rallies to endorse their candidate of choice. Increasingly politicians are relying on star-power to engage voters in their message and voters are responding, voting for one candidate over another because a Hollywood A-lister has endorsed a certain person for an important office. However, actors and actresses, though they can be smart and savvy people, are not trained in the political arena; they are often one-issue espousers and not briefed on the myriad of issues candidates have to address; and are often engaged by the candidate to be a draw rather than for their political experience or expertise. The question arises then, should candidates borrow star power to widen their voter base and are Hollywood opinions valid just because they have the power to speak and reach many ears, or should candidates for political office rely on their own messaging to get their ideas, passions and platforms across to voters?

Read and carefully consider these perspectives. Each suggests a particular way of thinking about the ways politicians and actors interact.

Perspective One	Perspective Two	Perspective Three
It is good that actors get involved in the political process since they can use their star power to engage voters who might otherwise never get involved in the process. Star power increases the general public's political awareness.	Actors and actresses command audiences and though people can listen to them, the Stars should encourage voters to do their own research and get involved locally with campaigns, so listeners are not following blindly and learn to formulate their own opinions based on what they believe in.	Actors and actresses are not politicians and their opinions are no more valid than any other private citizen's. Politicians should not use Hollywood voices to engage audiences, but rather hone and increase their messaging to reach the voter base themselves.

ESSAY 2

Essay Task

Write a unified, coherent essay about politicians and actors. In your essay, be sure to:

- Clearly state your own perspective on the issue and analyze the relationship between your perspective and at least one other perspective
- Develop and support your ideas with reasoning and examples
- Organize your ideas clearly and logically
- Communicate your ideas effectively in standard written English

Your perspective may be in full agreement with any of those given, in partial agreement or completely different.

ANALYSIS OF THE PROMPT

What is this prompt really asking?

In this prompt, the main question is about who influences public opinion. The nuance here is thinking through who has the right to tell people who to vote for in elections.

- *Just because certain people have influence on stage and screen, does that mean that their opinion matters in the political arena?*
- *Politicians sometimes ask if Hollywood superstars will share their stage so more people will come to see them, but is that the right use of their messaging power?*
- *The bottom line is that you have to decide who you want to hear from when you are choosing who to vote for and what or who do you think influences that decision?*

These are questions to ask when deconstructing your argument.

ESSAY 2

DECONSTRUCT THE ARGUMENT

PROS

Hollywood Stars should align themselves with politicians.

1. If an actor or actress has a strong opinion and wants to help raise money or get votes for a politician, then he or she should use their power to do so.

2. Actors and Actresses command viewers, which is a great help to a politician who is trying to get elected.

CONS

Hollywood Stars should not try to influence voters.

1. Actors and actresses are not politicians and may not understand all of the issues so they should not try to influence voters.

2. Actors and actresses' opinions are no more valid than anyone else's so they should stay out of politics.

From here, you should write a *thesis statement* that looks something like this:

"Stars of the stage and screen have the power to help politicians gain both funding and voters so they should align themselves with the politician they feel most expresses their viewpoints in order to increase audience attention and further the political message."

Or you can even go more simply than that:

"Actor involvement in American politics is a good thing as it engages the public on important political issues."

OUTLINE

Paragraph 1

Paragraph 2

Paragraph 3

Paragraph 4

Introduction and thesis statement

Tip: Be strong and specific with your hook – maybe mention a politician that makes heavy use of star power.

Topic sentence

Hollywood and stage stars can boost politicians' messages so that the public will vote for them.

Tip: Be very specific: in the U.S. the number of people who vote is low – perhaps actors can help raise awareness of the need to vote – especially with young voters who follow stars closely on various types of media.

Topic sentence

Politicians need funds to get elected and if a Hollywood superstar attends their fundraisers then more people will likely support that politician with money.

Tip: Perhaps you can choose an issue that you remember a politicial and an actor supporting – or even one that you support and then show how star power would boost it.

Counter argument topic sentence

Though some people think that starts of the stage and screen should not use their star power to get involved with politics, especially when they may not understand all the sides of various issues, actors and actresses' opinions are just as valid as anyone else's and they should use their star power to get good people elected into office.

Tip: You must try to show how/why someone would disagree with actors and actresses supporting politicians, but ultimately that the star power behind politicians is beneficial.

ESSAY 2

Paragraph 5

Conclusion and re-statement of thesis

Tip: When you restate the thesis, it has to be in slightly different words and you should finish strongly with a comment about the future or an idea that is most important, but the conclusion is NOT a place for new information.

This essay can easily be written from either perspective or using different examples. The key here is to focus on the argument you have deconstructed so you can stay focused on one idea per paragraph and be organized. Think through a time you heard an actor endorse a politician in a political advertisement. Was he or she believable? Why or why not? Each paragraph should have one to two examples and each example should be analyzed to connect it to the topic sentence or even the thesis statement before transitioning to the next paragraph.

ESSAY 2

SAMPLE ESSAY

Politics and Star Power

Donald Trump, the 45th president of the United States of America, was an actor, along with a career in real-estate. Ronald Reagan, a former American president, was an actor. Actors have climbed the social scale in America, all the way to the top political title. Actors and actresses have large amounts of influence in all areas of American life. While they appear in movies, television shows, radio shows, and streaming services, they also do much more. They take part in advertisements for things from cars to medicines. They appear on talk shows and sell books. Most significantly, they are active in all areas of American politics. They drive multiple issues and often appear on political stops in presidential campaigns. Actor involvement in American politics is a good thing as it engages the public on important political issues.

Introduction and thesis statement

Actor involvement in American politics is a good thing, as it increases voting and voter involvement across the nation. Voting across the nation is low compared to other developed nations. This droop in voting numbers is especially seen in midterm elections on non-presidential election years. It is also seen in younger age groups who often feel dissatisfied with the political climate. Actors are uniquely equipped to increase voting numbers in these areas. By attending primary election stops and advocating for a candidate's issues through speeches or just presence, actors can draw attention to the candidate and election and increase turnout. Additionally, actors are seen by and influential to younger voting audiences across the nation. So, they have the ability to use their influence and pop culture status to bring out the underrepresented populations within American youth. Actors can do this by appearing with politicians on shows, recording support videos, or appearing at stops. Thus, actor involvement in American politics is a good thing, as it increases voter turnout and engages the public on important political issues.

Supporting Paragraph: Example 1

Additionally, actor involvement in American politics is a good thing, as it draws attention to critical issues within the country. While actors and actresses often are unable to address the myriad of political issues in the country, they can attach themselves to one issue. Across the country, actors have brought attention to certain issues that, despite being against traditional American morals, go unnoticed or ignored. For example, Kim

Supporting Paragraph: More examples

ESSAY 2

Kardashian has attached herself to the issue of life sentences for those with unfair trials or circumstances. She has advocated for the release of many inmates publicly, and with the public's support, has seen much success. This stance by an actor helps draw attention to the blatant failures of incarceration in this country. Also, actors and actresses across the country have called attention to a certain issue in the past 4 years- immigration. Celebrities and actors have led the public outcry against the Trump administration's policy of separating children from families at the border. In addition, they led the movement against the inhumane situations children are kept in at the southern border. Thus, actor involvement in American politics is a good thing, as it draws attention to immoral government actions, and engages the public on important political issues.

Lastly, actor involvement in American politics is a good thing, as it provides a strong, beneficial example of civic responsibility and action. Children across the country grow up looking up to actors as the prime example of American citizens. By standing up against the government on issues they believe in, actors have inspired a generation of American citizens to do the same. Every day, actors and celebrities from Ellen De Generes to Robert Deniro set the standard of civil disobedience. Their stances and statements encourage and embolden the movements of the future. Parkland students have stood up against loose gun laws. Teachers have stood up for fair wages. Women have stood up for their rights under the Trump administration. Thus, actor involvement in American politics is a good thing, as it sets a strong example of civic responsibility for future generations and engages the public on important political issues.

Counter Argument with examples

However, another perspective on this issue is that actors should not be involved in the political process, as politicians should set their own messaging. Proponents of this viewpoint believe that actors and actresses steer political agendas left or right with their one-issue stances. But actor involvement does not heavily influence campaigns. Campaigns from the Sanders to Trump campaigns are not influenced unduly by actors and actresses- the actors and actresses choose a campaign that matches their views. Additionally, the public views of actors and actresses do not steer issues one way or another, as they encourage all to join the discussion and express their views. So, actor involvement is beneficial, as it attracts voters and introduces new arguments on issues.

ESSAY 2

In America, partisan politics have overtaken the agenda of the government. Liberal democrats spar with conservative republicans, with no middle ground. Congress is riddle with infighting, and progress is stalled by an acute lack of compromise. Personal insults are flung by both sides. American voters are becoming more disillusioned by our government than ever, and voting turnouts continue to fall. Actors and actresses have the unique ability to reverse or slow this downward spiral. Actor involvement in American politics is beneficial for all parties. By taking stances on issues and attending campaigns, actors have the ability to call attention to issues, raise turnout, and inspire the next generation to use their voices for change.

Conclusion

ESSAY **2**

This page is intentionally left blank.

ESSAY **3**

Free-Range Kids – Who Decides?

Analysis	**Solved**
Deconstruct	**Solved**
Outline	**Solved**
Sample Essay	**DIY**

	Reading time	Planning time	Writing time
Recommended	5 mins	5 mins	30 mins
Actual	_____	_____	_____

Free-Range Kids – Who Decides?

All parents have a goal to keep their children safe from harm, but every parent interprets that duty in different ways. Some parents choose to take their children to and from school, activities and play dates all the way through middle school or beyond. Other parents would prefer that their children learn to be independent and from a young age, allow them walk to various places such as school, friends' homes or other activities. People on both sides of the issue often cause heated debates, insisting that their point of view is the only one that could possibly be correct. The only outcome to such fiery discussion is harm to children by way of fights, police involvement and other negative outcomes, which is precisely what parents on both sides were looking to avoid.

Read and carefully consider these perspectives. Each suggests a particular way of thinking about who decides how to best keep children safe in their communities.

Perspective One	Perspective Two	Perspective Three
Parents of children twelve and under should always walk or drive their children everywhere - to and from school, to the park, activities and play dates. We live in a world of potential dangers and the only way to keep kids safe is to be with them at all times. These parents very strongly believe that vigilance is crucial.	Parents should have the choice to allow their children to be "free-range" and independent. Parents should be the ones to decide when their kids are ready to go places such as school, the park, the library or a play date unaccompanied. These parents very strongly believe that allowing their children to be independent fosters creative thinking and independence in other areas.	It is the job of society to protect children so any kids age twelve and under who are found by town officials to be walking around town unaccompanied should be brought home and the parents should be investigated for neglect.

ESSAY 3

Essay Task

Write a unified, coherent essay about free-range kids and community decision makers. In your essay, be sure to:

- Clearly state your own perspective on the issue and analyze the relationship between your perspective and at least one other perspective
- Develop and support your ideas with reasoning and examples
- Organize your ideas clearly and logically
- Communicate your ideas effectively in standard written English

Your perspective may be in full agreement with any of those given, in partial agreement or completely different.

ANALYSIS OF THE PROMPT

What is this prompt really asking?

The main question here is parental autonomy since the sides of the issue come down to who gets to decide when a child is able to function independently in the world. Some kids are ready to take responsibility for themselves when they are as young as 8 years old, but other children need time to mature before they are left alone or allowed to ride their bike to a friend's house. The trick here is the third perspective – not only are parents asking to decide for themselves, but some communities police how parents make those decisions. There have been countless stories about kids being picked up by police and taken home because they are biking alone to the library with parental permission and other similar scenarios. So, it is up to you, the writer, to decide not only which side of the issue is correct here, but also if communities should force parents on to one side or the other.

ESSAY 3

DECONSTRUCT THE ARGUMENT

PROS

Parents should be able to decide while moving around the community.

1. Parents are the people who know their children best, so they are fit to decide on their kids' maturity levels.

2. Parents should allow their children to go to friends' houses or the library on their own depending on the maturity of the child, but parents are also free to decline the opportunity to do so if they wish.

It is society's obligation to take care of its children, and that includes decisions about the relative safety of kids walking or biking alone without parents.

1. Members of society have to be very vigilant regarding the safety of their community streets, so everyone should watch out for everyone else.

2. Elected officials, police, and others should be able to tell parents when it is safe or unsafe to allow their children to move around town independently.

CONS

From here, you should write a *thesis statement* that looks something like this:

"Parents should be able to decide whether or not to send their children off to a friend's house or an activity under their own steam if they deem the child's maturity level high enough to handle the moves, and it is not the community's or the police force's job to make that decision for the parents."

ESSAY 3

OUTLINE

Paragraph 1

Introduction and thesis statement

Tip: Try to think as clearly as possible about the first few times your parents let you go out on your own and craft your thesis in light of your own experience.

Paragraph 2

Topic sentence

Parents know their child best and should be able to assess his or her maturity level.

Tip: Keep your eyes on the prize – it's the parents who know best. You are not necessarily coming down on the side of letting kids walk alone or not, but rather figuring out who gets to make that decision, parents or communities.

Paragraph 3

Topic sentence

Parents have the right to allow their appropriately mature child to be "free-range" and travel around town locally on their own steam, or they can decide to accompany their child to and from various events and activities.

Tip: Keep making your point – parents get to decide, not communities – or the opposite if you feel strongly about it.

Paragraph 4

Counter argument topic sentence

Though some people believe that local law enforcement and community leaders should fully protect children, Police forces, community activists and child protective services should take care before stepping in to accuse parents of neglect when those parents have made the conscious decision about the ability of their children to move around safely.

Tip: The counter-argument paragraph here is a little tricky because you have to stay focused on the decision makers, not the idea of children moving around alone.

ESSAY 3

Paragraph 5

Conclusion and re-statement of thesis

Tip: Once again think through your own first experiences with being on your own. Were you happy with your parents or not? This will inform your thesis statement and re-statement of the thesis.

This essay can easily be written from either perspective or using different examples. The key here is to focus on the argument you have deconstructed so you can stay focused on one idea per paragraph and be organized. Think about hypothetical examples of child neglect cases and how you might respond to those issues regarding parental rights and community responsibility. Your own experiences here are perfectly valid. Did your parents do the right thing by you, in your opinion?

ESSAY 3

SAMPLE ESSAY

Free-Range Kids – Who Decides?

_____

_____

_____

_____

_____

_____

_____ Introduction
and thesis
_____ statement

_____

_____

_____

_____

_____

_____

_____

_____ Supporting
Paragraph:
_____ Example 1

_____

_____

_____

_____

ESSAY 3

_____

_____

_____

_____

_____

_____

_____

_____

_____

_____

_____

_____

_____

Supporting
Paragraph:
More
examples

_____

_____

_____

_____

_____

_____

_____

_____

Counter
Argument
with
examples

ESSAY 3

_____

_____

_____

_____

_____

_____

_____

_____

_____

_____

_____

Conclusion _____

_____

_____

_____

_____

_____

_____

_____

_____

_____

_____

ESSAY 3

ESSAY **4**

Incentives for Charitable Donations

Analysis	**Solved**
Deconstruct	**Solved**
Outline	**Solved**
Sample Essay	**DIY**

	Reading time	Planning time	Writing time
Recommended	5 mins	5 mins	30 mins
Actual	_____	_____	_____

Incentives for Charitable Donations

There are many people who donate money to charity regularly and many others who donate their time and energy to their favorite charitable organizations. However, there are some people who do neither. In order to increase their pool of donors, of both time and money, sometimes organizations will try to incentivize people to give. For example, some public radio stations give away logo-bearing mugs or tote bags or even socks to people who give a certain amount of money every year. Schools regularly try to compel students to volunteer by offering them special service recognition in front of their peers. Though these types of incentives often achieve the goal, there are many people who believe that support in the form of financial donation or donation of time should be the reward in and of itself; people should give of their money and their time because it's a good thing to do, not just to get the reward.

Read and carefully consider these perspectives. Each suggests a particular way of thinking about offering incentives for charitable donations or volunteer hours.

Perspective One	Perspective Two	Perspective Three
People love to get gifts and recognition, so it is easy for societies, organizations and charities to give small gifts to their donors in return for their support. The donations could be in the form money or time and the gifts could be various types of the organization's "swag" or their names printed in publications.	Incentives are great for first-time donors or volunteers. The hope is that once the people give for the first time that they will be hooked on the feeling they get, knowing they have helped others and then will return on their own volition to volunteer again or donate again so the gift is only needed once.	People underestimate how good they will feel after giving their time or money to a worthy cause. Organizations who raise money or coordinate volunteers should not have to spend the charity's money in order to solicit donors' time and money. If they do, then the money raised does not go directly to the charity.

ESSAY 4

Essay Task

Write a unified, coherent essay about incentives for charitable donations and volunteerism. In your essay, be sure to:

- Clearly state your own perspective on the issue and analyze the relationship between your perspective and at least one other perspective
- Develop and support your ideas with reasoning and examples
- Organize your ideas clearly and logically
- Communicate your ideas effectively in standard written English

Your perspective may be in full agreement with any of those given, in partial agreement or completely different.

ANALYSIS OF THE PROMPT

What is the prompt really asking?

This prompt is more straightforward than some others because two of the perspectives match closely. One side says that it is perfectly fine to give incentive prizes to people who donate money or time to charitable organizations and the other side posits that a donation of time or money is a reward in itself, so no one needs a t-shirt or a mug with the name of a charity on it as a prize. The third perspective hedges a little bit though. The difference there allows that if a person can be convinced via an incentive prize to donate their time or money to an organization, then optimistically the donor will feel so good about his or her donation that after the first time, a prize will not be needed because the donor will feel great about his or her actions and will willingly repeat it without any incentive at all.

ESSAY 4

DECONSTRUCT THE ARGUMENT

PROS

Incentive prizes are a great way for organization to bring new donors or volunteers into their organization.

1. Organizations give prizes to their donors and volunteers as a way of saying thank you for their hard work or gift of time.

2. The gifts are low-cost and bought in bulk, so they have only a small effect on the bottom line of the charity.

3. Often, if the gift is good, donors and volunteers will repeat the action – and perhaps get a second gift.

4. Sometimes a second gift is not needed if the experience of giving is meaningful.

CONS

Organizations should not use prizes to incent volunteers or donors because being charitable is its own reward.

1. Donating money or volunteering for a charity that is meaningful for a person, makes him or her feel good about himself or herself, and that feeling carries them into repeating the actions – no gift needed.

2. Even if the gift is small, it still affects the bottom line a little bit and then less than 100% of the donation gets to the charity.

3. People who donate should do it willingly without reward.

From here, you should write a *thesis statement* that looks something like this:

"Giving donors and volunteers gifts in return for their charitable donations is a great idea because people enjoy "swag" and it brings people into the organization so they can further the mission of the organization effectively."

ESSAY 4

OUTLINE

Introduction and thesis statement

Tip: Have you ever gotten swag when volunteering? Or does a parent get swag from a donation? Be specific and mention those times if you can.

Topic sentence

Charities need donations of time and money and incentives are a great way to bring more people into the pool of donors.

> *Tip: Being specific is really important so discuss specifically HOW the incentives help bring in donors and volunteers. Think of a time it happened to you if you can.*

Topic sentence

The gifts charities give their donors and volunteers are small, like t-shirts and mugs, and do not greatly affect the bottom line of the charity; most of the money still goes to the mission of the organization.

> *Tip: This is a "don't worry" type of paragraph — the gifts are small, so you are assuring the reader that the charities are being ethical. Again, specifics are key if you can manage them.*

Counter argument topic sentence

While the gifts given by the charities by way of saying thank you are small, if people do not like the idea of an incentive gift, and they want to refuse the gift, then they are more than welcome to do so if their motivation is not affected by the gift.

> *Tip: The counter-argument here is quite strong but you must resist moving away from your point completely. Show that the other side exists but ultimately your side of the argument is superior. Be strong and specific about it.*

ESSAY 4

Paragraph 5

Conclusion and restatement of thesis

Tip: Your thesis has to be in different words than at the top of the essay and if possible, try to think of another example. If you cannot, then discuss how even considering this issue means that you are interested in donation and volunteerism, so the point is being charitable!

This essay can easily be written from either perspective or using different examples. The key here is to focus on the argument you have deconstructed so you can stay focused on one idea per paragraph and be organized. Think about situations where you have been offered an incentive to do something good for the environment or for someone else. For example, do you get paid to "work" in your place of worship? Or do you get a gift when you donate money to your favorite charity? Why or why not?

ESSAY 4

SAMPLE ESSAY

Incentives for charitable giving

_____

_____

_____

_____

_____

_____

_____ Introduction
and thesis
_____ statement

_____

_____

_____

_____

_____

_____

_____

_____

_____ Supporting
Paragraph:
_____ Example 1

_____

_____

_____

_____

ESSAY 4

_____

_____

_____

_____

_____

_____

_____

_____

_____

_____

_____

_____

_____

Supporting Paragraph: More examples

_____

_____

_____

_____

_____

_____

_____

_____

_____

ESSAY 4

Counter
Argument
with
examples

ESSAY 4

_____

_____

_____

_____

_____

_____

_____

_____

_____

_____

_____

_____

Conclusion

_____

_____

_____

_____

_____

_____

_____

_____

_____

_____

_____

ESSAY 4

ESSAY 5

Regulating the Size of Sugary Drinks

Analysis	**Solved**
Deconstruct	**Solved**
Outline	**Partly Solved**
Sample Essay	**DIY**

	Reading time	Planning time	Writing time
Recommended	5 mins	5 mins	30 mins
Actual	_____	_____	_____

Regulating the Size of Sugary Drinks

In May 2012, New York City Mayor Michael Bloomberg proposed what came to be known as the Sugary Drinks Portion Cap Rule. It was meant to be a citywide regulation that banned stadiums, delis, restaurants and other venues from selling any soda or juice in a cup larger than 16-ounces. In a country like the United States where bigger often means better, it was a sharp reversal on people's freedom to buy whatever they want. Mayor Bloomberg thought that by restricting the sizes of sugary drinks that people would take in less sugar and thus address an increasing problem of obesity in the city and nationwide. There was a sharp outcry from people who felt it was their right to buy large sized drinks if they wanted them, and not the city's business to tell them how to eat or drink. The resolution passed in the city's Board of Health, but was ultimately struck down by the State Supreme Court, which cited limits on freedom as most of its reasoning. The beverage companies were relieved that people in New York City could continue to buy any size drink they wanted and consume as much sugar as they wanted, regardless of the health consequences.

Read and carefully consider these perspectives. Each suggests a particular way of thinking about whether or not to regulate the sizes available for sugary drinks.

Perspective One	Perspective Two	Perspective Three
People have the right to eat and drink whatever they want regardless of the consequences. If a person wants to eat only cake and drink only soda all day every day, that is his choice and when he gets sick and becomes obese, it is only his problem.	It is the government's job to take care of people and the government should protect people from their baser instincts. If a person is overeating or drinking too much, then he or she should be stopped by the higher authorities and helped to make healthier choices.	Too many obese people in society is everyone's problem because when obesity rises, health care costs rise for everyone. The healthcare system is under pressure to take care of everyone regardless of ability to pay, which forces hospitals and insurance companies to raise rates for all people, whether obese or not.

ESSAY 5

Essay Task

Write a unified, coherent essay about regulating the size of sugary drinks. In your essay, be sure to:

- Clearly state your own perspective on the issue and analyze the relationship between your perspective and at least one other perspective
- Develop and support your ideas with reasoning and examples
- Organize your ideas clearly and logically
- Communicate your ideas effectively in standard written English

Your perspective may be in full agreement with any of those given, in partial agreement or completely different.

ANALYSIS OF THE PROMPT

What is the prompt really asking?

This controversy is very interesting because it has so many stakeholders. Individual people are affected but so are large beverage companies since they want people to spend more money on any sort of drinks. However, the reasoning behind the measure was that restricting drink sizes would force people to take in less sugar, ultimately resulting in lower obesity rates and less pressure on the New York City health systems. The health industrial complex could benefit from lowered obesity rates, possibly resulting in better care for people overall. So as you can see, this topic has many controversies surrounding it and must be approached with care.

ESSAY 5

DECONSTRUCT THE ARGUMENT

PROS

Cities should limit the sizes sugary drinks are available to consumers in order to force them to lower their sugar intake.

1. People will only spend money to buy only one drink, which is smaller, and end up consuming less sugar.

2. People who consume less sugar have lower obesity rates.

3. The city government has a responsibility to take care of its citizens – help them to be healthy and lower the overall obesity rate.

CONS

Limiting sizes of drinks sold in restaurants will not significantly help people lower their sugar intake.

1. People will end up buying more than one drink, therefore going around the regulation and end up with the same amount of sugar.

2. People should have the freedom to eat and drink what they want regardless of the health effects.

3. It is not government's responsibility to tell people what to eat or drink.

From here, you should write a *thesis statement* that looks something like this:

"The government of the City of New York should limit the size of all sugary drinks available to the public in order to reduce citizens' sugar intake and the obesity rate in the city, which will ultimately reduce health care costs overall."

OUTLINE

Introduction and thesis statement

Tip: Think of a time when you bought a huge drink. How would you feel if you couldn't purchase it? That will inform your thesis statement, and give you a strong, specific hook for your essay.

Topic sentence

If the city government can limit the size of drinks available then people will buy fewer drinks that contain large amounts of sugar, which will lower their sugar intake considerably.

Tip: Show the effects of sugar on the body and then tie the sugar to the drinks — be specific!

Topic sentence

If people are able to lower their sugar intake, then they will lower their chances of becoming obese, so ultimately the sugar limit could lower those obesity rates city-wide.

Tip: Here's the next step so you need to be as logical as possible — link the sugar to the drinks to obesity to an epidemic. Be clear on why this is a big problem that can be addressed in this specific manner.

Counter argument topic sentence

Tip: In general, with a counter-argument, your job is to turn away from your own idea for a moment and then turn back to it. Here you need to specifically show the other side and then show how it's incorrect. Specifics are important here because the issue is so controversial.

_____

_____

Paragraph 1

Paragraph 2

Paragraph 3

Paragraph 4

ESSAY 5

_____

_____

Conclusion and restatement of thesis

Tip: Your thesis statement must be re-stated strongly in different words and conclude with an idea for the future, but without truly new information. It's tricky!

This prompt has many facets to it so that it will take a skillful writer to make sure that every paragraph is unified around one, over-arching idea. For example, some students will reason that large drinks lead to high sugar intake, which leads to obesity, which leads to high healthcare costs. That might be correct, but it is too much for one paragraph. Students must take special care to go slowly and limit each paragraph to one idea and then at the end perhaps tie some of the ideas together. Just remember, one idea per paragraph! Explain and analyze your points fully and the essay will turn out well.

ESSAY 5

SAMPLE ESSAY

Regulating the Size of Sugary Drinks

Introduction
and thesis
statement

Supporting
Paragraph:
Example 1

ESSAY 5

_____

_____

_____

_____

_____

_____

_____

_____

_____

_____

_____

_____

_____

Supporting
Paragraph:
More
examples

_____

_____

_____

_____

_____

_____

_____

_____

ESSAY 5

Counter
Argument
with
examples

ESSAY 5

_____

_____

_____

_____

_____

_____

_____

_____

_____

_____

_____

Conclusion

_____

_____

_____

_____

_____

_____

_____

_____

_____

_____

ESSAY 6

Golf: Sport or Game?

Analysis	Solved
Deconstruct	Solved
Outline	Partly Solved
Sample Essay	DIY

	Reading time	Planning time	Writing time
Recommended	5 mins	5 mins	30 mins
Actual	_____	_____	_____

Golf: Sport or Game?

Almost 150,000 students, both male and female (Statista.com) in American high schools are involved with a golf team. Many high schools across the United States have varsity golf teams, but despite the fact that the International Olympic Committee has deemed golf as a sport which was played at the 2016 games, a controversy exists about whether or not golf in general should be named a "sport" or a "game." Those who want to call it a sport note that golfers have agents and endorsements just like athletes in other sports. Those who resist calling golf a sport say that if you can play it while drinking lemonade, then it must not be a true sport.

Read and carefully consider these perspectives. Each suggests a particular way of thinking about whether golf should be considered a sport or a game.

Perspective One	Perspective Two	Perspective Three
Golfers practice and train hundreds of hours a year to compete in tournaments that are held all over the world. Of course, golf is a sport.	While golf could be a sport or a game, the fact remains that it is beloved by millions across the globe. It is played competitively at thousands of high schools and colleges and helps people stay relatively fit well past middle age.	In 2008 Golfer Tiger Woods played – and won – a tournament while having a stress fracture in his left leg. Any game where that can be done is just that – a game – not a sport per se.

Essay Task

Write a unified, coherent essay about whether golf is a sport or a game. In your essay, be sure to:

- Clearly state your own perspective on the issue and analyze the relationship between your perspective and at least one other perspective
- Develop and support your ideas with reasoning and examples
- Organize your ideas clearly and logically
- Communicate your ideas effectively in standard written English

Your perspective may be in full agreement with any of those given, in partial agreement or completely different.

ANALYSIS OF THE PROMPT

What is the prompt really asking?

On the surface, this seems to be simply asking whether or not golf is a sport or not. However, there are many layers to the question, not the least of which is how to define a sport. Since Tiger Woods became a professional golfer (after a strong amateur career) in 1996, the world of golf has expanded exponentially, and has included large endorsement deals never before seen in the game. It is up to you to decide if one star player and increased funding should allow the game of golf to be categorized as a sport. In an era where poker and corn-hole games are shown on ESPN, this is not a frivolous question.

ESSAY 6

DECONSTRUCT THE ARGUMENT

PROS

Golf has made hundreds of otherwise unknown men and women into sports heroes, so of course golf is a sport.

1. Golf does take a certain amount of athleticism and strength and coordination.

2. The coordination it takes to swing a golf club is twice that of sports like soccer or lacrosse.

3. Golfers who are in good physical shape do better at golf, which is like any other sport.

4. Golfers do get injured and it affects their play – often sidelining them for weeks if not months, with injuries to the back or hip.

CONS

Golf has no defense and no teamwork so it cannot be labeled as a true sport.

1. Golf is something that can be done at any age, unlike other sports where the younger an athlete is means the stronger his or her performance will be.

2. There is no defensive action in the game of golf, which disqualifies it from being a sport. All other sports have to defend a goal or a net or something to prevent others from scoring.

3. The number of calories burned is 1/3 less than if a person played soccer for an hour instead of golfing.

From here, you should write a *thesis statement* that looks something like this:

"While golf is fun and interesting to both play and watch, since it does not require a strong sense of athleticism, it is not technically a sport."

ESSAY 6

OUTLINE

Paragraph 1

Introduction and thesis statement

Tip: Though it will be difficult to come down on one side of the argument, you have to choose a side – or a perspective at least. Really think through why you feel the way you do.

Paragraph 2

Topic sentence

Golfers can come in all shapes and sizes, tall and short, fat and thin, unlike in real sports.

Tip: Try to think through golf game, a golf commercial or even a product endorsed by a golfer. That will help you figure out the specific things you want to point out about the golfers.

Paragraph 3

Topic sentence

Tip: This is where your expertise might come in handy – relating golf to another sport. Maybe you feel more confident in the other sport and can compare strongly and specifically.

_____

_____

_____

_____

_____

Paragraph 4

Counter argument topic sentence

Tip: What does it take to be a golfer? What does it take to play other sports? Think through what skill and talent mean, and what is innate and what can be learned.

ESSAY 6

_____

_____

_____

_____

_____

Paragraph 5

Conclusion and restatement of thesis

Tip: Re-state your thesis strongly in light of what you have proven. Be as specific as possible and think of anything that points to the future of golf.

While on the surface this seems like a straightforward argument on which we just have to take a side, the way the argument is crafted takes careful consideration. When making a case, please remember to state your ideas firmly and use as many examples as you can to prove the point. Sports are a huge part of the fabric of American life so most people will be able to bring in specific arguments and examples to make their case.

SAMPLE ESSAY

Golf as a Sport or a game?

_____

_____

_____

_____

_____

_____

Introduction
and thesis
statement

_____

_____

_____

_____

_____

_____

_____

Supporting
Paragraph:
Example 1

_____

_____

_____

_____

ESSAY 6

_____

_____

_____

_____

_____

_____

_____

_____

_____

_____

_____

_____

Supporting
Paragraph:
More
examples

_____

_____

_____

_____

_____

_____

_____

_____

ESSAY 6

_____

_____

_____

_____

_____

_____

_____

_____

_____

_____

_____

_____

_____

Counter
Argument
with
examples

_____

_____

_____

_____

_____

_____

_____

_____

_____

_____

_____

ESSAY 6

_____

_____

_____

_____

_____

_____

_____

_____

_____

_____

_____

Conclusion _____

_____

_____

_____

_____

_____

_____

_____

_____

_____

ESSAY 6

ESSAY **7**

"Sin" Taxes

Analysis	Solved
Deconstruct	Solved
Outline	Partly Solved
Sample Essay	DIY

	Reading time	Planning time	Writing time
Recommended	5 mins	5 mins	30 mins
Actual	_____	_____	_____

"Sin" Taxes

Taxes on commodities are very common, and specifically taxes on unhealthy commodities date back to the Revolutionary War Period in the U.S. Tobacco and alcohol taxes raised money for both the Confederate and Union Armies during the Civil War. The purpose of such taxes is to dissuade use of the item in question, but the people who impose the taxes are well aware of the nature of humans to want things that are deemed via taxes to be "sinful" but are also expressly legal. For example, there have been numerous proposals in various cities to place a tax on sugary beverages, considering they contribute to the obesity problem in the U.S. If an excise or "flat", per-item tax is levied then perhaps there would be more money for jurisdictions to fight the effects of social problems such as poverty and income inequality. Are such taxes correct or are they just a way to further promote bad behavior?

Read and carefully consider these perspectives. Each suggests a particular way of thinking about whether or not unhealthy or unwise behavior should be taxed.

Perspective One	Perspective Two	Perspective Three
The Federal Government should levy taxes on items or activities that are "sinful" such as gambling, cigarettes, alcohol and even sugary drinks because the higher prices might dissuade people from the item or activity.	The Federal Government should rely on localities to tax so-called sinful behavior that is appropriate for that jurisdiction. For example, Rhode Island has casinos and can charge people a tax on their winnings, which add to the state coffers so that the money is available for other types of social programs.	Both the Federal and Local Governments should not levy taxes on anything they deem "sinful" since it is not the government's job to tell people how to behave. If people want to drink alcohol, smoke cigarettes or gamble or even drink hundreds of calories of sugar, then it is their private business.

Essay Task

Write a unified, coherent essay analyzing the idea of taxing behaviors. In your essay, be sure to:

- Clearly state your own perspective on the issue and analyze the relationship between your perspective and at least one other perspective
- Develop and support your ideas with reasoning and examples
- Organize your ideas clearly and logically
- Communicate your ideas effectively in standard written English

Your perspective may be in full agreement with any of those given, in partial agreement or completely different.

ANALYSIS OF THE PROMPT

What is the prompt really asking?

Much of the meat of this prompt is beyond the financial realm. It is not just about whether or not the item should be taxed, but if people should be allowed to misbehave if they want to.

- *Does the government have the right to hold people to a higher standard via financial means?*

Traditionally the smoking rates go down when jurisdictions levy a tax of up to $1 per pack of cigarettes, but there are enough people who are willing to pay the tax in order to keep smoking, so it is not a large deterrent. As of yet, no jurisdiction has been able to place a tax on sugary drinks even though the cost of obesity-related complications has put a strain on the health care system and sugary drinks are a part of the problem. People do not want their freedom restricted in general, or they are willing to pay for it. What do you think?

ESSAY 7

DECONSTRUCT THE ARGUMENT

PROS

The government should be able to levy a tax on things that are inherently unhealthy, such as gambling or cigarettes.

1. The so-called "sin" taxes do dissuade people even slightly from bad behavior. Smoking rates lower when cigarette taxes go up.

2. Some of the money raised from such taxes can go to fund social programs such as welfare or certain health education programs.

3. Traditionally, if a candidate running for office, whether local or federal, proposes such a tax, it will be popular with voters.

CONS

People should have the freedom to consume or do whatever they want without having a tax.

1. The tax only serves to make people who want to behave badly to want to do it more. It doesn't fully eliminate the behavior.

2. The rate at which the items are taxed has been relatively small, not enough to fully fund prevention or abatement programs.

3. The tax is subjective. Who gets to say what is good behavior and what is not? Why are some harmful things taxed and not others?

From here, you should write a *thesis statement* that looks something like this:

"Taxes on commodities such as gambling, smoking or even sugary drinks make sense because they might dissuade usage and the tax will also help pay for relevant social programs in the U.S.

ESSAY 7

OUTLINE

Paragraph 1

Introduction and thesis statement

Tip: Your specifics here need to be as strong as possible. What do you believe? Can you give an example of something you would or would not purchase if it was taxed?

Topic sentence

Paragraph 2

Tip: Use details from your own experience of anything that is forbidden that you decided to do anyway or purchase anyway. Since you are not of age to buy alcohol or cigarettes, what can you envision yourself doing in the future?

_____

_____

_____

_____

_____

Topic sentence

Paragraph 3

Tip: Strongly tying the benefits of the tax to specific programs makes the paragraph stronger, so try to be as detailed as you can.

_____

_____

_____

_____

ESSAY 7

Counter argument topic sentence

Tip: This is a classic freedom conundrum. Who gets to decide what is taxed and what is not? Give your opinion and try to be as strong and specific as possible. What do you feel now and what might you think in the future when controversial items are within your own grasp?

_____

_____

_____

_____

_____

Conclusion and restatement of thesis

Tip: Discuss morality and how it can or cannot be regulated – and who gets to potentially regulate it. Re-state the thesis in different words.

_____

_____

_____

_____

_____

This essay has the potential to be very interesting depending on the point of view you take with it. The writer has to be careful to combine what is right and wrong with the potential health hazards with the economics of taxes and social programs. If you take the opposite tack to this one, then it behooves you to be very strong in your desire to choose freedom over government oversight of safety. Think carefully and find specific examples.

ESSAY 7

SAMPLE ESSAY

"Sin" Taxes

_____

_____

_____

_____

_____

_____

_____   Introduction
and thesis
statement

_____

_____

_____

_____

_____

_____

_____

_____   Supporting
Paragraph:
Example 1

_____

_____

_____

_____

ESSAY 7

_____

_____

_____

_____

_____

_____

_____

_____

_____

_____

_____

_____

_____

Supporting
Paragraph:
More
examples

_____

_____

_____

_____

_____

_____

_____

_____

ESSAY 7

_____

_____

_____

_____

_____

_____

_____

_____

_____

_____

Counter
Argument
with
examples

_____

_____

_____

_____

_____

_____

_____

_____

_____

_____

ESSAY 7

_____

_____

_____

_____

_____

_____

_____

_____

_____

_____

_____

Conclusion

_____

_____

_____

_____

_____

_____

_____

_____

_____

_____

_____

_____

_____

ESSAY 7

ESSAY **8**

Advertising Prescription Drugs

Analysis	**Solved**
Deconstruct	**Solved**
Outline	**DIY**
Sample Essay	**DIY**

	Reading time	Planning time	Writing time
Recommended	5 mins	5 mins	30 mins
Actual	_____	_____	_____

Advertising Prescription Drugs

In 2017, Harvard Health Publishing reported that advertisements touting prescription drugs rose from $3.2 billion to $5.2 billion between 2012 and 2015. The United States is one of only a handful of countries in the world that allows the prescription drug makers to market their wares directly to consumers. The ads are meant to be controlled by the Food and Drug Administration (FDA), but their regulators only see the ads once they are released, not before the public has access to them, which means that incorrect information could potentially reach the public before the FDA has seen and evaluated the advertisement for correctness and quality. Proponents of prescription drug advertising note that people become informed of potential treatments for their problems and then go see their physicians, improving overall health. Opponents of direct-to-consumer marketing of prescription drugs complain that the chance of misinformation is high and common problems such as hair loss or facial wrinkles are becoming "medicalized" because more people seek prescription relief due to the ads.

Read and carefully consider these perspectives. Each suggests a particular way of thinking about whether or not drug companies should advertise directly to consumers.

Perspective One	Perspective Two	Perspective Three
It is good that drug companies can advertise directly to consumers because it gives potential patients the knowledge about treatment, side effects and even the illness itself, all within a broadcast medium familiar to them that they are already using and trust.	Drug companies should not advertise directly to consumers because there is a chance that the potential patient could misunderstand the information and be misinformed about their conditions and the ability of medications to treat them.	It is okay for drug companies that make prescription drugs to market directly to consumers if the FDA is given more specific, prior access to the advertisements as a regulatory body to ensure that all information in the advertisements is correct and aimed only at helping potential patients, not only making sales.

ESSAY 8

Essay Task

Write a unified, coherent essay about advertising prescription drugs directly to consumers. In your essay, be sure to:

- Clearly state your own perspective on the issue and analyze the relationship between your perspective and at least one other perspective
- Develop and support your ideas with reasoning and examples
- Organize your ideas clearly and logically
- Communicate your ideas effectively in standard written English

Your perspective may be in full agreement with any of those given, in partial agreement or completely different.

ANALYSIS OF THE PROMPT

What is the prompt really asking?

In this prompt, it is about more than just advertising; it is also about the FDA's ability to be a proper regulator of the advertisements. If the FDA does not see the ads before they reach the public, there is a strong chance of misinformation, which could potentially lead to accidents with the drugs. It is possible to take a stand on the side of denying the public access to advertisements about the drugs, of course, but regulation must be addressed at some point in the essay. It is okay to mention the way the advertisements always end with a long, quickly-read litany of side effects that might harm users, and in fact such a specific detail might add a note of interest to the piece.

- *Why do the advertisers use that particular method of listing potential problems?*
- *Writers might consider what the issues are surrounding that list of disclaimers and why it exists in the first place – what does it have to do with the drugs vis-a-vis regulation?*

ESSAY 8

DECONSTRUCT THE ARGUMENT

PROS

Drug advertisements are good for consumers as long as they are regulated by the FDA.

1. Patients who see ads for prescription drugs are more likely to see their doctors for treatment of a specific ailment, which the FDA wants.

2. The FDA knows that patients who see advertisements for prescription drugs are more likely to take medication correctly, as directed by their doctors.

3. Sales of prescription drugs rise via direct to consumer advertisements and that money can go into research into other new treatments, which get FDA approval.

CONS

Regardless of regulation, advertisements of prescription drugs directly to the consumer are harmful.

1. Advertisements encourage over-medication, particularly with drugs for mood disorders and sleep issues.

2. The advertisements of prescription drugs put pressure on healthcare providers to over-prescribe due to more requests for medicine.

3. The advertisements "medical-ize" normal signs of aging, such as hair loss and wrinkles and encourage medical treatment for some general life conditions.

Thesis statement

_____

_____

_____

ESSAY 8

OUTLINE

Introduction and thesis statement

Tip: Use a hook that perhaps describes a drug commercial you saw.

_____

_____

_____

_____

Paragraph 1

Topic sentence

Tip: Don't forget to focus on regulations here like the question is asking. Move forward with the description of the ad you saw and then what might happen if the ad is or is not regulated.

_____

_____

_____

_____

Paragraph 2

Topic sentence

Tip: Here's the financial side – ads equal purchases within theory allows the drug companies to do more research. Help the reader make that connection strongly and specifically.

_____

_____

_____

_____

Paragraph 3

ESSAY 8

Paragraph 4

Counter argument topic sentence

Tip: Here's where you can describe in detail what would happen on the opposite side of the argument – but make sure the reader comes to understand that your side is much better!

_____

_____

_____

_____

_____

Paragraph 5

Conclusion and restatement of thesis

Tip: If you used a specific example of a drug commercial at the top, you might mention it here again. Re-state your thesis strongly.

_____

_____

_____

_____

_____

Given this sticky situation, addressing both sides of the argument along with the idea of regulation will strengthen the argument. If a writer can give a personal example, then it will be even better. Do you know anyone who takes medication for a non-medical reason? Have you ever seen one of those ads and can you discuss what you did or did not like about it? As usual, be as specific as you can.

SAMPLE ESSAY

Advertising Prescription Drugs

_____

_____

_____

_____

_____

_____   Introduction
                                                      and thesis
_____   statement

_____

_____

_____

_____

_____

_____

_____

_____   Supporting
                                                      Paragraph:
_____   Example 1

_____

_____

_____

_____

ESSAY 8

_____

_____

_____

_____

_____

_____

_____

_____

_____

_____

_____

_____

_____

Supporting
Paragraph:
More
examples

_____

_____

_____

_____

_____

_____

_____

_____

_____

ESSAY 8

Counter
Argument
with
examples

_____

_____

_____

_____

_____

_____

_____

_____

_____

_____

_____

Conclusion

_____

_____

_____

_____

_____

_____

_____

_____

_____

_____

_____

ESSAY 8

ESSAY 9

Buying Bottled Water

Analysis	**Solved**
Deconstruct	**Partly Solved**
Outline	**DIY**
Sample Essay	**DIY**

	Reading time	Planning time	Writing time
Recommended	5 mins	5 mins	30 mins
Actual	_____	_____	_____

Buying Bottled Water

A 2013 report by *Slate* notes that Americans spend 300 times the cost of a gallon of tap water in order to buy a gallon of bottled water. The report additionally says that Americans are the largest consumers of bottled water, and most of the water sold in the U.S. is in single serving bottles, not gallons, which drives the price up further. The price of refillable water bottles is not cheap, but ultimately helps reduce the amount of plastics filling landfills or worse, littering our parks and cities. According to the *New York Times*, in 2014, San Francisco passed a bill banning the sale of bottled water under 21 ounces in public spaces. The city upgraded water fountains and water-filling stations across the city. Opponents of such measures say that people will resort to buying sugary drinks if water is unavailable, which just creates a different type of problem. They also note that such measures hurt the small vendors in city parks that might want to sell bottled water at a premium price.

Read and carefully consider these perspectives. Each suggests a particular way of thinking about whether or not single-serving water bottles should be available for purchase.

Perspective One	**Perspective Two**	**Perspective Three**
Buying a refillable bottle in which to carry water is a one-time expense that pays for itself over and over again with the opportunity to fill it in public places all over the city and countryside. Families that are willing to carry water for each member can save upwards of $1000 yearly.	Buying a refillable water bottle makes sense for the environment because it saves space in landfills and helps cities and parks avoid litter issues.	If cities ban the sale of bottled water under 21 ounces then there will be many harmful effects, including people who will buy sugary drinks like soda or juice instead, which increases the risk of obesity, a different type of problem for municipalities to face.

Essay Task

Write a unified, coherent essay about buying single-serve bottles of water. In your essay, be sure to:

- Clearly state your own perspective on the issue and analyze the relationship between your perspective and at least one other perspective
- Develop and support your ideas with reasoning and examples
- Organize your ideas clearly and logically
- Communicate your ideas effectively in standard written English

Your perspective may be in full agreement with any of those given, in partial agreement or completely different.

ANALYSIS OF THE PROMPT

What is the prompt really asking?

This problem is very straightforward because there are clear sides to be taken. Some people prefer not to carry a water bottle with them and prefer to buy bottled water to drink whenever and wherever they are thirsty. Others do not mind the heft of a water bottle and trust they will find a filling station in their travels around town. The people who come down on the side of selling the bottles often cite freedom as one issue – they should be able to buy what they want and not be regulated by the government as to what they can purchase and where. Environmentalists will use pollution and the inability of plastics to be fully recycled as evidence of the harm water bottles potentially cause. It is up to you to examine your own ideals and discuss a side of the issue – or find a creative middle ground about which to write.

ESSAY 9

DECONSTRUCT THE ARGUMENT

PROS

The sale of bottled water should be banned in public places if the bottles are under 21 ounces – i.e. meant for single use.

1. Bottled water costs significantly more than tap water if people can fill a reusable bottle.

2. Reusable water bottles are a one-time expense and filling them is not often free at stations across towns and cities.

_____
_____
_____
_____
_____
_____
_____
_____

CONS

Bottled water in single-use bottles should be available for sale wherever people are likely to need it.

1. Restricting the sale of water bottles hurts small vendors who regularly boost their incomes at large, public events with the sale of water.

2. It limits personal freedom if people cannot buy water at the size they prefer whenever they want it.

_____
_____
_____
_____
_____
_____
_____
_____

Thesis statement

_____

_____

_____

OUTLINE

Introduction and thesis statement

Tip: When you write a hook to use before your thesis statement, make sure that it is specific – perhaps you can think of a time you bought a water bottle and were glad to have it.

_____

_____

_____

_____

Topic sentence

Tip: This is the economic side to the issue, not the environmental side, so try to think of the problem from the point of view of a private vendor.

_____

_____

_____

_____

Topic sentence

Tip: Have you ever been unable to buy something you wanted? Write about that example specifically.

_____

_____

Paragraph 1

Paragraph 2

Paragraph 3

ESSAY 9

_____

_____

_____

_____

Paragraph 4

Counter argument topic sentence

Tip: Here's where you need to connect issues. If you can't buy water, you will buy what's available, which might be sugary and add calories to your diet. What would you do if you could not buy water somewhere? Be specific!

_____

_____

_____

_____

Paragraph 5

Conclusion and restatement of thesis

Tip: Think of how you see this issue playing out in the future when you end the essay.

_____

_____

_____

_____

In addressing this prompt, writers should be careful to construct their argument in such a way that appeals to readers and helps them understand the real meat of the issue of cost and the environment, while relating it tangentially to the obesity epidemic in the U.S. Any specific details or personal experiences that writers can relate would be an extra advantage to helping the issue really come alive off the page.

ESSAY 9

SAMPLE ESSAY

Buying Bottled Water

_____

_____

_____

_____

_____

_____ Introduction
and thesis
_____ statement

_____

_____

_____

_____

_____

_____ Supporting
Paragraph:
_____ Example 1

_____

_____

_____

_____

ESSAY 9

_____

_____

_____

_____

_____

_____

_____

_____

_____

_____

_____

_____

_____

_____

_____

_____

Supporting
Paragraph:
More
examples
_____

_____

_____

_____

_____

_____

_____

_____

_____

ESSAY 9

Counter
Argument
with
examples

ESSAY 9

_____

_____

_____

_____

_____

_____

_____

_____

_____

_____

_____

Conclusion _____

_____

_____

_____

_____

_____

_____

_____

_____

_____

ESSAY 9

ESSAY 10

A Computer for Every Student

Analysis	**Solved**
Deconstruct	**Partly solved**
Outline	**DIY**
Sample Essay	**DIY**

	Reading time	Planning time	Writing time
Recommended	5 mins	5 mins	30 mins
Actual	_____	_____	_____

A Computer for Every Student

School districts across the U.S. are implementing 1:1 computer programs whereby each student is issued a school-owned and supported laptop computer for use during not only the school day, but in some cases, at home as well. Proponents of the program argue that students need preparation for being digital citizens and also for the type of collaborative work required of students in college and in the workplace. Those against the programs cite the expense of not only the devices but also of the personnel needed to maintain the machines. All school districts are looking for a way to promote equality of access to technology but is a 1:1 computer program the way to do it?

Read and carefully consider these perspectives. Each suggests a particular way of thinking about 1:1 computer programs in schools.

Perspective One	**Perspective Two**	**Perspective Three**
School districts in the United States should not invest in a computer for every student because the money would be better spent elsewhere, like for infrastructure updates to school buildings, teacher salaries or support personnel for students in crisis.	If the schools have buy-in from teachers and can support the technology staff in their work, then it is worth the investment to have a computer for every student since it promotes equity in the classroom among students who might be of different economic and/or racial backgrounds.	Every school district in the United States should invest without reservation in having a computer available for each student because it is the best way to prepare students for the demands of college and the workplace beyond, including collaborative tools, digital citizenship and problem solving abilities.

Essay Task

Write a unified, coherent essay about 1:1 computer programs in schools. In your essay, be sure to:

- Clearly state your own perspective on the issue and analyze the relationship between your perspective and at least one other perspective
- Develop and support your ideas with reasoning and examples
- Organize your ideas clearly and logically
- Communicate your ideas effectively in standard written English

Your perspective may be in full agreement with any of those given, in partial agreement or completely different.

ANALYSIS OF THE PROMPT

What is the prompt really asking?

It might be hard for students looking at this prompt to separate themselves from the idea of wanting to have a computer for themselves if they don't already have one, but they must try to think about it in terms of what is best for students and what is best for school systems.

- *If you had your own laptop all the time, would you use it responsibly or would you install apps on it to communicate with your pals?*
- *Would you use it to collaborate on a research project?*

Computers are extremely expensive items – so most school systems have to make decisions on which students will get the machines and which ones are too young. They are not only expensive to buy, but they are also expensive to maintain and someone has to be in charge of all of that maintenance. In a high school of 1000 students, there might have to be two technology specialists whose salaries have to be paid. Think carefully whether or not the computer is worth the expense and where you would like to see your school district adopt a program like this one. Computers vs. tablets is a completely different debate, as is reading on a tablet vs. books, so be careful to stick to the topic at hand.

DECONSTRUCT THE ARGUMENT

PROS

There should be one computer for every student in schools.

1. The younger the students learn about computers, the better off they will be, including the care and maintenance of the machines.

_____

_____

_____

_____

_____

_____

_____

_____

_____

_____

_____

_____

_____

CONS

Students do not each need a computer and the money would be better spent on other programs at the schools.

1. If students are truly disadvantaged in various ways, there are services and programs that they need such as free or reduced lunches and the money spent on computers could better support those types of programs.

_____

_____

_____

_____

_____

_____

_____

_____

_____

_____

ESSAY 10

Thesis Statement

_____

_____

_____

_____

OUTLINE

Introduction and thesis statement

Tip: Try to use your imagination and think through what it would look like if every student in every classroom had a laptop open. You might describe that for your hook.

_____

_____

_____

_____

Paragraph 1

Topic sentence

Tip: Give examples of how equity and confidence might be boosted via computers. Everyone would have the opportunity to learn. Everyone would feel good about their ability to learn.

_____

_____

_____

_____

Paragraph 2

Topic sentence

Tip: This paragraph is asking you to think about the softer skills students would learn, so be as strong and specific as you can be about additional perks of the potential program.

_____

_____

Paragraph 3

ESSAY 10

_____

_____

_____

_____

Paragraph 4

Counter argument topic sentence

Tip: A program like this has drawbacks, of course, but your job is to mention them and then note that the drawbacks are not sufficient to kill the program. Make the reader see your point as superior through examples and descriptions.

_____

_____

_____

_____

Paragraph 5

Conclusion and restatement of thesis

Tip: You might finish with a stress on the future of education!

_____

_____

_____

_____

Students must really consider their position on this issue since it would be easy to say every student needs a computer because they want their own computer. There are many arguments against this type of program. By approaching the prompt with a middle-ground type of thesis that leans in one direction, you can easily describe examples of potential successes or detractions. Be strong in your beliefs and give clear and explained examples. Try to be as logical and descriptive as you can.

SAMPLE ESSAY

A Computer for Every Student

Introduction and thesis statement

Supporting Paragraph: Example 1

ESSAY 10

_____

_____

_____

_____

_____

_____

_____

_____

_____

_____

_____

_____

_____

_____

Supporting
Paragraph:
More
examples

_____

_____

_____

_____

_____

_____

_____

_____

_____

ESSAY 10

_____

_____

_____

_____

_____

_____

_____

_____

_____

_____ Counter
Argument
with
_____ examples

_____

_____

_____

_____

_____

_____

_____

ESSAY 10

_____

_____

_____

_____

_____

_____

_____

_____

_____

_____

_____

Conclusion

_____

_____

_____

_____

_____

_____

_____

_____

_____

_____

ESSAY 10

ESSAY **11**

School Uniforms

Analysis	**Solved**
Deconstruct	**Partly Solved**
Outline	**DIY**
Sample Essay	**DIY**

	Reading time	Planning time	Writing time
Recommended	5 mins	5 mins	30 mins
Actual	_____	_____	_____

School Uniforms

According to the National Center for Education Statistics, in 2015 21% of public school districts in the U.S. require their students to wear uniforms to class. This is a jump of 9% over the prior 15 years. The schools that do require the uniforms note that students can concentrate better in class, and the differences between the lower and higher income students is much less apparent if they are all dressed the same way. In contrast, those opposed to compulsory uniforms in schools say that the uniforms restrict freedom of expression and also promote conformity rather than individuality in schools. Other parts of the debate rage around crime rates and school spirit either rising or falling based on the wearing or not wearing of uniforms in school. What do you think about having all students in a given school dressed alike, or at least similarly?

Read and carefully consider these perspectives. Each suggests a particular way of thinking about school uniforms.

Perspective One	Perspective Two	Perspective Three
Public School districts in the United States should require students to wear some sort of uniform because it promotes a sense of unity among students.	Public school districts in the U.S. should not require students to wear uniforms because it restricts students' freedom in various ways, including the freedom to express their creativity via their wardrobe and be an original individual in all matters of school life.	School districts should be allowed to choose whether or not to require uniforms based on their population of students but need to take into account their population of students, including their diversity on many fronts including both race and economics.

ESSAY 11

Essay Task

Write a unified, coherent essay about school uniforms. In your essay, be sure to:

- Clearly state your own perspective on the issue and analyze the relationship between your perspective and at least one other perspective
- Develop and support your ideas with reasoning and examples
- Organize your ideas clearly and logically
- Communicate your ideas effectively in standard written English

Your perspective may be in full agreement with any of those given, in partial agreement or completely different.

ANALYSIS OF THE PROMPT

What is the prompt really asking?

This is a very interesting prompt for a student to consider since it has the power to affect him or her directly. Very rarely are issues black and white and this one too, has nuance to discover. In order to answer this question fully, students must think about economic as well as freedom-oriented issues relating to dress codes. Students in one school rarely originate from one economic group so it is up to you to decide if the uniforms can erase some of the signs of economic differences in homes. Think through the idea of freedom. Maybe you express your individuality via your clothing; there are many people who signal their membership in various groups in schools based on their apparel. Hoodies and t-shirts can be representative of groups and if students are required to wear certain types of shirts and pants or skirts, then those affiliations become less and less important.

- *How else might uniforms affect students in school?*
- *Do they create a sense of belonging for everyone? Why or why not?*

ESSAY 11

DECONSTRUCT THE ARGUMENT

PROS

Students in every school district in the U.S. should be required to wear some type of uniform.

_____
_____
_____
_____
_____
_____
_____
_____
_____
_____
_____
_____
_____
_____
_____
_____

CONS

Students should not be required to wear a uniform to schools in the U.S. though dress codes are proper.

_____
_____
_____
_____
_____
_____
_____
_____
_____
_____
_____
_____
_____
_____
_____
_____

ESSAY 11

From here, you should write a *thesis statement* that looks something like this:

_____

_____

_____

OUTLINE

Introduction and thesis statement

Tip: In your hook, feel free to use the statistics listed in the start of the prompt!

_____

_____

_____

_____

Paragraph 1

Topic sentence

Tip: Think about the idea of creativity and what the uniforms would do to it. Be specific about the limitations.

_____

_____

_____

_____

Paragraph 2

Topic sentence

Tip: This paragraph would address the decision-makers. Parents have a right to decide — try to think of examples of when parents insist on things and all parents do not decide the same way.

_____

_____

Paragraph 3

ESSAY 11

_____

_____

_____

_____

_____

Paragraph 4

Counter argument topic sentence

Tip: As in all counter-argument paragraphs, you must show the opposite side, but then show how your idea is the best, most sensible one. Be specific and describe the uniforms carefully.

_____

_____

_____

_____

Paragraph 5

Conclusion and restatement of thesis

Tip: What do you imagine is the future of uniforms in the U.S.? How might that affect freedom?

_____

_____

_____

_____

Students really do need to decide which side of the argument they want to support and then firmly stand on it. This is not one of those prompts that can be smoothed over with a middle ground. Hopefully you will be able to weigh the evidence carefully and choose a side. The details must be strong and convincing so that it seems like all sides of the argument have been assessed. Your descriptions of uniforms and how they affect students in various types of classrooms will be crucial to making your arguments specific. Be clear and be strong in your words and thoughts.

ESSAY 11

SAMPLE ESSAY

School Uniforms

Introduction and thesis statement

Supporting Paragraph: Example 1

ESSAY 11

_____

_____

_____

_____

_____

_____

_____

_____

_____

_____

_____

_____

_____

_____

Supporting
Paragraph:
More
examples

_____

_____

_____

_____

_____

_____

_____

_____

ESSAY 11

Counter
Argument
with
examples

ESSAY 11

_____

_____

_____

_____

_____

_____

_____

_____

_____

_____

_____

Conclusion _____

_____

_____

_____

_____

_____

_____

_____

_____

_____

ESSAY 11

ESSAY **12**

Free Tuition at State Universities

Analysis	**Solved**
Deconstruct	**Partly Solved**
Outline	**DIY**
Sample Essay	**DIY**

	Reading time	Planning time	Writing time
Recommended	5 mins	5 mins	30 mins
Actual	_____	_____	_____

Free Tuition at State Universities

The College Board reports that between the 2008-2009 school year and the 2018-2019 school year, tuition and fee costs rose by $930 (in 2018 dollars) at public two-year colleges, by $2,670 at public four-year institutions, and by $7,390 at private nonprofit four-year colleges and universities. This number does not include room and board prices. The cost of attending college has become out of reach for many people. Students are increasingly reaching for loans, both from the schools and private loans and the costs of paying back those loans is also becoming crippling as more students graduate with mammoth sums of debt. Some politicians propose that college tuition at state institutions should be free to students but there are many issues surrounding that proposal, including questions about how state budgets can manage the cost, and what the proposal will do to enrollments at those colleges.

Read and carefully consider these perspectives. Each suggests a particular way of thinking about free tuition at state universities.

Perspective One	Perspective Two	Perspective Three
States should find a way to make tuition free to students in their jurisdiction because those students will stay in the state and make the investment in talented students worthwhile.	Free tuition is a misnomer because students tend to forget that room and board costs money as well and they might not be able to afford the rest of the assorted costs of college beyond tuition anyway.	States should not make state universities completely tuition free because it will cost taxpayers in that state billions of dollars without any hope of the money being repaid, and so far there has not been a plan on how to fund the costs without pulling money from other valid programs.

ESSAY 12

Essay Task

Write a unified, coherent essay about free tuition at state universities. In your essay, be sure to:

- Clearly state your own perspective on the issue and analyze the relationship between your perspective and at least one other perspective
- Develop and support your ideas with reasoning and examples
- Organize your ideas clearly and logically
- Communicate your ideas effectively in standard written English

Your perspective may be in full agreement with any of those given, in partial agreement or completely different.

ANALYSIS OF THE PROMPT

What is the prompt really asking?

Given the option of course everyone would like to have a free education! However, what students often forget is that there are other costs associated with going to college beyond just tuition, including room and board and other fees. The prompt is asking you to figure out where you stand on the issue of "free" college. If the state pays, then likely taxes with rise into the stratosphere. But some people say that everyone deserves the opportunity to go to college and this is the only way to make it happen.

- *Consider the fact of who attends college – does everyone need a college degree to fulfill their dreams – or even get a job? What do you think?*

DECONSTRUCT THE ARGUMENT

PROS

_____
_____
_____
_____
_____
_____
_____
_____
_____
_____
_____
_____
_____
_____
_____
_____
_____
_____

It is not the state's job to pay for a student's desired college education after having paid for the prior 12 years.

_____
_____
_____
_____
_____
_____
_____
_____
_____
_____
_____

CONS

ESSAY 12

From here, you should write a *thesis statement* that looks something like this:

_____

_____

_____

_____

OUTLINE

Introduction and thesis statement

Tip: In your introduction, be clear on what fees and costs you are addressing with the idea of "free".

_____

_____

_____

_____

Paragraph 1

Topic sentence

Tip: Even if you do not want to discuss tax rates and other government funding, you have to address the ways the payments to the universities might be made if tuition is free. Try to be specific in your ideas.

_____

_____

_____

_____

Paragraph 2

Topic sentence

Tip: This is often unforeseen, and making this argument is difficult. Think of how much living expenses affect someone's ability to go to college and be as specific as you can. Describe.

_____

_____

Paragraph 3

ESSAY 12

Counter argument topic sentence

Tip: In this complex paragraph, you have to show how the opposite of your argument is true but less compelling than your argument. Think through examples and specifics of how and why your argument is the best one.

Paragraph 4

Conclusion and restatement of thesis

Tip: When you conclude here you can take the statistics from the top of the prompt and try to weave them into the conclusion. Trying to address the future here is a little bit fuzzy.

Paragraph 5

This essay will take some real thinking because it affects every student either directly or indirectly. Even if you have student loans in the end, an education is more than a piece of paper; it is a priceless entry ticket into the world of knowledge creation that must be taken with the utmost of seriousness. Should every person have a college degree or are there other options for students who have varying interests? Who should bear the cost of educating this nation's students? This is the real question for your consideration.

SAMPLE ESSAY

Free Tuition at State Universities

_____

_____

_____

_____

_____

_____

Introduction
and thesis
statement

_____

_____

_____

_____

_____

_____

_____

_____

Supporting
Paragraph:
Example 1

_____

_____

_____

_____

_____

ESSAY 12

_____

_____

_____

_____

_____

_____

_____

_____

_____

_____

_____

_____

_____

_____

_____

_____

Supporting
Paragraph:
More
examples

_____

_____

_____

_____

_____

_____

_____

_____

ESSAY 12

_____

_____

_____

_____

_____

_____

_____

_____

_____

_____

_____

Counter
Argument
with
examples

_____

_____

_____

_____

_____

_____

_____

_____

ESSAY 12

_____

_____

_____

_____

_____

_____

_____

_____

_____

_____

_____

Conclusion _____

_____

_____

_____

_____

_____

_____

_____

_____

_____

ESSAY 12

ESSAY 13

Honor Codes

Analysis	Solved
Deconstruct	DIY
Outline	DIY
Sample Essay	DIY

	Reading time	Planning time	Writing time
Recommended	5 mins	5 mins	30 mins
Actual	_____	_____	_____

Honor Codes

Even though Harvard University has been in existence for close to 400 years, it was not until Fall of 2015 that the revered institution implemented an official Honor Code, which came after four years of work and study regarding the best way to do it for their specific population. Since its inception, students who are accused of academic dishonesty are referred to the honor council and it is the work of the council, which is comprised of a mix of students, faculty and deans, to determine if a violation of the code took place and then what sanctions to impose. In contrast, the University of Virginia (UVA) has had an honor code since 1842, in accordance with its founder, Thomas Jefferson. With the advent of the Internet, however, cases of academic dishonesty have skyrocketed and it is incumbent upon universities across the U.S. to investigate whether their practices surrounding academic dishonesty are working to prevent actions that violate the code and if the sanctions for doing so are in line with the crimes.

Read and carefully consider these perspectives. Each suggests a particular way of thinking about honor codes.

Perspective One	Perspective Two	Perspective Three
Honor Codes at various universities have the power to impose sanctions that could prove ruinous to a student's academic career, thus limiting career options, so honor councils need to be judicious in meting out punishment.	Asking students to sign an honor code statement at the start of every exam or at the top of every essay acts as a deterrent to academic dishonesty in most cases, so honor councils often do not need to impose sanctions.	Dishonesty of any sort should not be tolerated and Honor Councils at universities should punish students for violations right to the limit of the code so that students understand the value of honesty, both academic and otherwise and will act to be strong advocates of the truth.

ESSAY 13

Essay Task

Write a unified, coherent essay about honor codes in schools. In your essay, be sure to:

- Clearly state your own perspective on the issue and analyze the relationship between your perspective and at least one other perspective
- Develop and support your ideas with reasoning and examples
- Organize your ideas clearly and logically
- Communicate your ideas effectively in standard written English

Your perspective may be in full agreement with any of those given, in partial agreement or completely different.

ANALYSIS OF THE PROMPT

What is the prompt really asking?

This prompt is quite tricky because it is discussing the topic of honor codes from the standpoint of sanctions and their efficacy. Think about what would happen if your teacher caught you copying from a website directly into your essay. In many schools the paper would be given a zero if it was a first offense. If it was not a first offense, then perhaps a student would be given an "F" for the class. In college semesters are only about 15 weeks, so the courses are changing often enough that the one bad grade makes a difference.

- *What are your thoughts on honor codes and academic dishonesty?*
- *If a student is feeling tired or lazy is there ever an excuse to take a short cut to finish an essay or cheat on an exam?*

Think about the consequences of those actions. In an essay responding to this prompt, students must address the idea of the sanctions on honor code violations (which are different for every university) and if they work to prevent or deter those violations.

ESSAY 13

DECONSTRUCT THE ARGUMENT

PROS

CONS

ESSAY 13

From here, you should write a *thesis statement* that looks something like this:

_____

_____

_____

_____

OUTLINE

Introduction and thesis statement

Tip: Does your high school have an honor code? If so, you might start by describing it. If not then, explain why?

_____

_____

_____

_____

Topic sentence

Tip: The best way to address this idea is with a specific example. Think of a time someone in your school committed academic dishonesty. It does not matter if he or she got caught, rather that you can describe the specific incident.

_____

_____

_____

_____

Topic sentence

Tip: Give an example of how honor code enforcement actually prevents violations. Try to be specific and detailed.

_____

_____

_____

Paragraph 1

Paragraph 2

Paragraph 3

ESSAY 13

_____

_____

_____

_____

Counter argument topic sentence

Tip: This is asking you to think of an idea about when honor codes are not useful, the opposite of your thesis. It's okay to give a specific example, and then you can turn it back to why your idea is better.

_____

_____

_____

_____

Conclusion and restatement of thesis

Tip: In the future, you are going to go to college. How is high school honor code enforcement different?

_____

_____

_____

_____

Paragraph 4

Paragraph 5

This should be an interesting topic for students to tackle because it will relate directly to their lives and interests, especially as they move forward into college. Honor codes are in place at most universities and most places have an office of academic integrity or an honor council or something of that nature to monitor potential violations of the code and then mete out punishment if it is found that the code has been violated. Are the punishments effective? Do they deter further action to violate the code? Think through your opinion carefully to see if you agree or disagree and why or why not.

ESSAY 13

SAMPLE ESSAY

Honor Codes

Introduction
and thesis
statement

Supporting
Paragraph:
Example 1

ESSAY 13

_____

_____

_____

_____

_____

_____

_____

_____

_____

_____

_____

_____

_____

_____

_____

Supporting
Paragraph:
More
examples
_____

_____

_____

_____

_____

_____

_____

_____

_____

ESSAY 13

_____

_____

_____

_____

_____

_____

_____

_____

_____

_____

Counter
Argument
with
examples

_____

_____

_____

_____

_____

_____

_____

_____

_____

ESSAY 13

_____

_____

_____

_____

_____

_____

_____

_____

_____

_____

_____

Conclusion _____

_____

_____

_____

_____

_____

_____

_____

_____

_____

ESSAY 13

ESSAY **14**

Arts Funding in Schools

Analysis	**DIY**
Deconstruct	**DIY**
Outline	**DIY**
Sample Essay	**DIY**

	Reading time	Planning time	Writing time
Recommended	5 mins	5 mins	30 mins
Actual	_____	_____	_____

Arts Funding in Schools

The National Endowment for the Arts, in their 2012 study, found that among students from a low socio-economic background, "Eighth graders who had high levels of arts engagement from kindergarten through elementary school showed higher test scores in science and writing than did students who had lower levels of arts engagement over the same period" (https://www.arts.gov/sites/default/files/Arts-At-Risk-Youth.pdf). Yet despite these numbers, education in art, theater and music is always the first item that gets cut when budgets run tight in school districts in the U.S. Similarly, Federal Budget proposals suggest trimming the funding for the National Endowment for the Arts or Public broadcasting when something needs to be cut. In wealthier school districts, the parents often fund the gaps in arts education because the benefits, including elevated test scores, better class performance and college entry advantages, are so clear. If study after study shows that all students, regardless of backgrounds, benefit tremendously from exposure to the arts and training in the arts, why is funding for these programs at such a high risk of elimination?

Read and carefully consider these perspectives. Each suggests a particular way of thinking about funding arts programs and classes in schools.

Perspective One	**Perspective Two**	**Perspective Three**
Students across the U.S. can gain exposure to music, art and theater outside of school, so if budgets are tight in school districts, arts funding should be cut because other academic programs and/or programs like free lunch for underprivileged students are more important.	As students fall under more and more pressure to succeed academically, often arts education is their lifeline to a bit of sanity in their lives. Music or art class might be a place where students get to shine and be happy when the constant pressure gets to be too much. Success in the arts is just as important as other academic areas.	The studies linking arts education with success in other academic areas are too strong to ignore and funding for the arts should not only remain stable, but also increase if we are to support especially low-income students in their bid to achieve in other areas like math and science. Brain development in all areas happens in concert.

ESSAY 14

Essay Task

Write a unified, coherent essay funding arts programs in schools. In your essay, be sure to:

- Clearly state your own perspective on the issue and analyze the relationship between your perspective and at least one other perspective
- Develop and support your ideas with reasoning and examples
- Organize your ideas clearly and logically
- Communicate your ideas effectively in standard written English

Your perspective may be in full agreement with any of those given, in partial agreement or completely different.

ANALYSIS OF THE PROMPT

What is this prompt really asking?

_____
_____
_____
_____
_____
_____
_____
_____
_____

ESSAY 14

DECONSTRUCT THE ARGUMENT

PROS

CONS

From here, you should write a *thesis statement* that looks something like this:

_____

_____

_____

_____

OUTLINE

Introduction and thesis statement

Tip: Give examples of arts in your school and what would happen if they disappeared

_____

_____

_____

_____

Paragraph 1

Topic sentence

Tip: Be as specific as possible regarding how the arts effect students. Give examples from your school if you can. Relate the arts classes to mainstream classes.

_____

_____

_____

Paragraph 2

Topic sentence

Tip: This paragraph is aimed at community. In your school, how is community created? Try to relate the idea of community to arts classes, leading to other communities.

_____

_____

Paragraph 3

ESSAY 14

_____

_____

_____

_____

Paragraph 4

Counter argument topic sentence

Tip: This is your counter-argument, so you want to make sure your point still stands out while addressing the opposite side, but you still have to be strong and specific. Think through the true effects of funding the arts.

_____

_____

_____

_____

Paragraph 5

Conclusion and restatement of thesis

Tip: Arts are an integral part of a community; make sure to state the case as you see fit but with examples that are clear and specific.

_____

_____

_____

_____

If you participate in any type of art yourself then you likely have a strong opinion on this issue. Make sure that your ideas are clear and calm and ordered, not let out in a rush. As usual, you have to organize each paragraph around one clear idea and then give examples before moving to the next paragraph – the next idea. It is great to use your own experiences as examples as long as you are able to analyze them fully and show how they prove the point you are trying to make. Be strong and specific in your ideas.

ESSAY 14

SAMPLE ESSAY

Funding for Arts Programs

_____

_____

_____

_____

_____

_____

_____   Introduction
                                                                    and thesis
_____   statement

_____

_____

_____

_____

_____

_____

_____

_____   Supporting
                                                                    Paragraph:
_____   Example 1

_____

_____

_____

_____

ESSAY 14

_____

_____

_____

_____

_____

_____

_____

_____

_____

_____

_____

_____

_____

_____

Supporting
Paragraph:
More
examples _____

_____

_____

_____

_____

_____

_____

_____

ESSAY 14

_____

_____

_____

_____

_____

_____

_____

_____

_____

_____

_____ Counter
_____ Argument
with
_____ examples

_____

_____

_____

_____

_____

_____

_____

_____

_____

ESSAY 14

_____

_____

_____

_____

_____

_____

_____

_____

_____

_____

_____

Conclusion

_____

_____

_____

_____

_____

_____

_____

_____

_____

ESSAY 14

ESSAY **15**

Traditional Books vs. Reading Devices

Analysis	DIY
Deconstruct	DIY
Outline	DIY
Sample Essay	DIY

	Reading time	Planning time	Writing time
Recommended	5 mins	5 mins	30 mins
Actual	_____	_____	_____

Traditional Books vs. Reading Devices

As early as 2008, award winning technology writer Nicholas Carr noted differences in the way people were reading based on their use of the Internet and various devices with screens rather than traditional books. He also cites text on a screen affecting humans' ability to think as he says, "Our ability to interpret text, to make the rich mental connections that form when we read deeply and without distraction, remains largely disengaged" (*Is Google Making Us Stupid?* The Atlantic, July/August 2008). More than ten years later, debates still rage about the differences screens make on students' ability to read and think. This debate has come up more recently since school districts are interested in giving students tablets on which to read instead of issuing them traditional textbooks. Arguments for the tablets include easy of transport and the ability to update contents, but arguments for traditional textbooks are financial in nature and also note the ease of reading. What do you think schools should do, stay with traditional textbooks or issue tablet readers to students?

Read and carefully consider these perspectives. Each suggests a particular way of thinking about including advertisements in school environments.

Perspective One	**Perspective Two**	**Perspective Three**
Studies have shown that students who read traditional textbooks retain more information and are able to deeply process that information in a stronger, clearer way. Reading on a tablet or screen of any sort is a different type of skill and often students get more distracted when reading on a tablet than from a traditional book.	Tablets have many advantages over textbooks because they can be easily updated and students have better access to new information faster than with traditional textbooks. The tablets are more environmentally friendly and help to save on paper and even teacher handouts.	Textbooks are better than tablets because they are less expensive and take no maintenance; they also limit the excuse factor because students cannot claim they did not complete a reading or research assignment because their textbook crashed.

ESSAY 15

Essay Task

Write a unified, coherent essay about textbooks vs. e-books. In your essay, be sure to:

- Clearly state your own perspective on the issue and analyze the relationship between your perspective and at least one other perspective
- Develop and support your ideas with reasoning and examples
- Organize your ideas clearly and logically
- Communicate your ideas effectively in standard written English

Your perspective may be in full agreement with any of those given, in partial agreement or completely different.

ANALYSIS OF THE PROMPT

What is this prompt really asking?

_____

_____

_____

_____

_____

_____

_____

ESSAY 15

DECONSTRUCT THE ARGUMENT

PROS

_____
_____
_____
_____
_____
_____
_____
_____
_____
_____
_____
_____
_____
_____
_____
_____
_____
_____

_____
_____
_____
_____
_____
_____
_____
_____
_____
_____
_____
_____
_____
_____
_____
_____
_____
_____

CONS

From here, you should write a *thesis statement* that looks something like this:

_____

_____

_____

_____

OUTLINE

Introduction and thesis statement

Tip: It is okay to use the quote or a statistic from the prompt in your hook.

_____

_____

_____

Paragraph 1

Topic sentence

Tip: It might be good here to give specific examples from your own experience with learning with various types of texts. Be clear on how you really feel but use language that is not only focused on you – perhaps include the reader with "we".

_____

_____

_____

Paragraph 2

Topic sentence

Tip: Maybe you can give specific examples of times technology didn't work for you and times you had a problem with a traditional book. Which was more painful?

_____

_____

_____

_____

Paragraph 3

ESSAY 15

Paragraph 4

Counter argument topic sentence

Tip: Don't forget – in your counter argument paragraph, you address the opposite side of an issue, but you have to make sure the reader still understands that your point of view is best. Specific examples help.

_____

_____

_____

_____

Paragraph 5

Conclusion and restatement of thesis

Tip: Go back to the description of your experience here or the idea of the prompt at the top in order to make sure the essay is tied together strongly.

_____

_____

_____

_____

_____

At this point in time, is tempting to think that tablets are a "cool" way of learning for students, but the reality is that tablets have their own issues. Schools would have to make a very large investment if they want to replace all textbooks with tablets. Similar to having many computers in schools, there would have to be staff on hand in schools to perform maintenance on malfunctioning tablets. There are other considerations regarding the potential for tablets to malfunction, including reduced battery life over time and the ability of a tablet to be hacked from outside. All in all, there are many considerations one must think about before coming down on one side of this issue. Are you a technologist or a traditionalist?

ESSAY 15

SAMPLE ESSAY

Traditional Books vs. Reading Devices

_____

_____

_____

_____

_____

_____

_____ Introduction
and thesis
_____ statement

_____

_____

_____

_____

_____

_____

_____

_____ Supporting
Paragraph:
_____ Example 1

_____

_____

_____

_____

ESSAY 15

_____

_____

_____

_____

_____

_____

_____

_____

_____

_____

_____

_____

_____

Supporting
Paragraph:
More
examples   _____

_____

_____

_____

_____

_____

_____

_____

ESSAY 15

_____

_____

_____

_____

_____

_____

_____

_____

_____

_____

Counter
Argument
with
examples

_____

_____

_____

_____

_____

_____

_____

_____

ESSAY 15

_____

_____

_____

_____

_____

_____

_____

_____

_____

_____

_____

_____

Conclusion _____

_____

_____

_____

_____

_____

_____

_____

ESSAY 15

ESSAY 16

Teachers and Debt

Analysis	**DIY**
Deconstruct	**DIY**
Outline	**DIY**
Sample Essay	**DIY**

	Reading time	Planning time	Writing time
Recommended	5 mins	5 mins	30 mins
Actual	_____	_____	_____

Teachers and Debt

Very often student debt is a tricky topic, and never more so than for K-12 teachers. Teachers today have to invest tens of thousands of dollars into their educations and the financial rewards of teaching are not commensurate with the debt payments most educators have to incur in order to be certified to teach in many states. A 2019 study by the Center for American Progress reports that the problem disproportionately affects college graduates of Latino or African American descent, which then affects teacher diversity nationwide. Teachers of color are desperately needed across the United States so that all students can find a role model in schools who might look like them. Solutions to ever-increasing levels of debt incurred by our nation's educators are desperately needed, especially as educational requirements for teachers (masters' degrees, continuing education units) continue to rise disproportionately with salaries, pricing many top students out of the field of education.

Read and carefully consider these perspectives. Each suggests a particular way of thinking about teachers and student debt loans.

Perspective One	**Perspective Two**	**Perspective Three**
Student loans are a fact of life in the U.S. now, given the high costs of college. It doesn't matter what field students enter after their university years; all students should have to pay back their debt in full even teachers who are in public service, no matter where they teach.	States should have programs like the one in Boston that allow federal loan forgiveness if new teachers (who must be fully certified including a masters' degree) dedicate their first few years of teaching to needy, underserved city schools.	Universities should dedicate special funding for students who intend to enter the teaching profession, so those students do not incur debt. There is no higher calling than to prepare our next generation and schools should make it easy to make the choice to do it.

Essay Task

Write a unified, coherent essay about teachers and student loans. In your essay, be sure to:

- Clearly state your own perspective on the issue and analyze the relationship between your perspective and at least one other perspective
- Develop and support your ideas with reasoning and examples
- Organize your ideas clearly and logically
- Communicate your ideas effectively in standard written English

Your perspective may be in full agreement with any of those given, in partial agreement or completely different.

Planning sheets and Answer sheets can be downloaded from the **Online Resource** section of this book on
www.vibrantpublishers.com

ESSAY 16

This page is intentionally left blank.

ESSAY **17**

Zoos: yea or nay?

Analysis	**DIY**
Deconstruct	**DIY**
Outline	**DIY**
Sample Essay	**DIY**

	Reading time	Planning time	Writing time
Recommended	5 mins	5 mins	30 mins
Actual	_____	_____	_____

Zoos: yea or nay?

Zoos have existed since ancient Egyptian times and people have always been interested in the care and keeping of so-called "exotic" animals. In modern times, most zoos not only keep animals, but also extensively study them so we can understand various habits, habitats and even socialization. In extreme examples, zoos are the only places where endangered species can mate and replenish the population, even if it's just bit-by-bit. Zoos educate their visitors daily on the various animals they keep, how those animals live and should be treated. However, some people insist that it is cruel to have zoos and keep animals in captivity. They say that zoos can be both physically and psychologically harmful to animals and the knowledge we gain does not justify the treatment. Are zoos necessary or are they just a nod to man's vanity at being at the top of the food chain?

Read and carefully consider these perspectives. Each suggests a particular way of thinking about zoos.

Perspective One

Zoos across the U.S. and the globe fulfill an important mission in the understanding of our planet because if animals are in captivity, scientists can study their habits, environments and even their socialization for clues on how to keep our world at its most functional.

Perspective Two

The ability to study animals does not justify the existence of zoos since it is often psychologically as well as physically harmful to keep animals in captivity. There is story after story of animals dying after being brought to zoos and not being allowed to live as nature intended.

Perspective Three

While zoos perform an important function in the education of people about our complex planet and its eco systems, there should be standards of care for animals so that the habitats in which they are kept closely mirror their natural habitats and the animals are physically and psychologically safe.

ESSAY 17

Essay Task

Write a unified, coherent essay about zoos. In your essay, be sure to:

- Clearly state your own perspective on the issue and analyze the relationship between your perspective and at least one other perspective
- Develop and support your ideas with reasoning and examples
- Organize your ideas clearly and logically
- Communicate your ideas effectively in standard written English

Your perspective may be in full agreement with any of those given, in partial agreement or completely different.

Planning sheets and Answer sheets can be downloaded from the **Online Resource** section of this book on **www.vibrantpublishers.com**

ESSAY 17

This page is intentionally left blank.

ESSAY 18

Car Seats for Kids' Programming

Analysis	**DIY**
Deconstruct	**DIY**
Outline	**DIY**
Sample Essay	**DIY**

	Reading time	Planning time	Writing time
Recommended	5 mins	5 mins	30 mins
Actual	_____	_____	_____

Car Seats for Kids' Programming

After school programs and day-camps are staples of care for the children of busy, working parents. Mothers and fathers who work long hours can be sure that their children are safe and entertained and educated via programs such as after-school or summertime Karate and Art Classes that are not necessarily on the grounds of the schools. Often these programs have their own transportation and pick up the children from school or home and some even bring them home in the evening, sometimes using large vans, not buses. These vans are not held to the same safety standards as buses with regards to cocooning children inside and having certain types of seats, and most often the kids are using seatbelts meant for adults. If one of these vans is in an accident, the seat belt might do as much damage to small bodies as the accident itself since the belt is not positioned correctly for children's heights and weights. There is not a state in the U.S. that requires these types of programs to use car seats or boosters for its transportation, but given the potential for harm, should the programs be required to properly safeguard kids in their vehicles?

Read and carefully consider these perspectives. Each suggests a particular way of thinking about car seats for after school and summer programs

Perspective One	Perspective Two	Perspective Three
Most states in the U.S. have strict laws regarding children and car seats, involving complex calculations of the child's age, weight and height. School buses are specially designed to keep children safe and children should not be in a vehicle at all if they are not buckled in safely.	It is the parents' responsibility as much as the programs' responsibility to keep their children safe so if they want their child to ride in the institutional transportation, they should provide the proper car seat or booster to the program in order to keep their child safe. Everyone should share in this all-important mission of keeping children as safe as possible on the road.	After school and summer programs have limited budgets because they are trying to be responsive to working parents' need for affordable programs for their children and they put the most money into the program itself. They should not have to worry about additional transportation costs when most kids are just traveling short distances between school, the program and home.

Essay Task

Write a unified, coherent essay car seats and after school programming. In your essay, be sure to:

- Clearly state your own perspective on the issue and analyze the relationship between your perspective and at least one other perspective
- Develop and support your ideas with reasoning and examples
- Organize your ideas clearly and logically
- Communicate your ideas effectively in standard written English

Your perspective may be in full agreement with any of those given, in partial agreement or completely different.

Planning sheets and Answer sheets can be downloaded from
the **Online Resource** section of this book on
www.vibrantpublishers.com

ESSAY 18

This page is intentionally left blank.

ESSAY 19

Teacher Tenure

Analysis	**DIY**
Deconstruct	**DIY**
Outline	**DIY**
Sample Essay	**DIY**

	Reading time	Planning time	Writing time
Recommended	5 mins	5 mins	30 mins
Actual	_____	_____	_____

Teacher Tenure

Tenure, the sought-after ideal for teachers, means the ultimate in job security. K-12 teachers with tenure are generally guaranteed a job in their school district for their entire working life, until they choose to retire. In the U.S. most states have a system of tenure that allows teachers to apply for this golden opportunity somewhere between their second and fifth year of teaching. Different states have different systems. In a country that does not pay their teachers well for the all-important job they are doing, tenure is one of the benefits of employment along with state health insurance and almost always a good retirement plan. However, some people insist that a "job for life" situation makes even good teachers a little lazy and less responsive to students and parents. Teachers with tenure might not work as hard as teachers who have not yet attainted that standard and it is virtually impossible to legally fire a teacher who is already tenured. In this environment of a lack of qualified teachers across the U.S., is tenure the right way to go to protect teachers?

Read and carefully consider these perspectives. Each suggests a particular way of thinking about teacher tenure.

Perspective One	Perspective Two	Perspective Three
Tenure is a terrible idea since it allows mediocre teachers to continue teaching, it makes it impossible to fire bad teachers, and it creates complacency among teacher who may lose their motivation to performs well in the classroom.	Tenure is the best way to protect teachers from politically motivated firings, as well as from districts firing more experienced teachers to hire less expensive and less experienced teachers. Tenure is the only way to protect the good teachers and give them the respect and compensation they so richly deserve.	Tenure is a fine way to protect teachers and motivate people to become teachers, but the system has to be reformed so that teachers cannot get tenure until the district is sure that the teacher is a viable employee long term. Tenure should not be an option before the teacher has been on the job for ten or more years.

Essay Task

Write a unified, coherent essay about teacher tenure. In your essay, be sure to:

- Clearly state your own perspective on the issue and analyze the relationship between your perspective and at least one other perspective
- Develop and support your ideas with reasoning and examples
- Organize your ideas clearly and logically
- Communicate your ideas effectively in standard written English

Your perspective may be in full agreement with any of those given, in partial agreement or completely different.

Planning sheets and Answer sheets can be downloaded from the **Online Resource** section of this book on **www.vibrantpublishers.com**

ESSAY 19

This page is intentionally left blank.

ESSAY 20

Pokemon Go – Friend or Foe?

Analysis	DIY
Deconstruct	DIY
Outline	DIY
Sample Essay	DIY

	Reading time	Planning time	Writing time
Recommended	5 mins	5 mins	30 mins
Actual	_____	_____	_____

Pokemon Go – Friend or Foe?

According to the online publication Business of Apps, in March 2019, Pokemon Singapore reported that the game Pokemon Go hit the 1 Billion mark for total downloads since its release in 2016. The popular game, released Niantic, along with characters created by Nintendo (which has an ownership stake in Niantic), has soared in marketshare, still capturing 85% of the gaming market as of mid-2019, adds Business of Apps. Gamers who love it report that they are out and about constantly in order to "capture" the Pokemon characters and they have created communities and meet-ups based on the game. Those gamers also say that due to the game's culture of getting out and about, former couch-potatoes who love Pokemon Go end up getting out more and more, improving their health significantly. Detractors of the game note that accidents happen because the gamers have their noses in their screens, and that sacred, quiet places like Arlington National Cemetery and the 9/11 Memorial in New York City have had to ask the gamers not to play while on the premises because they interrupt the contemplative nature of those places. Given the popularity of the game worldwide, should we consider it a boon or a bust to society in general?

Read and carefully consider these perspectives. Each suggests a particular way of thinking about the viability of Pokemon Go.

Perspective One	Perspective Two	Perspective Three
The game Pokemon Go is a menace to society because it causes accidents when people are too busy playing and they cross streets without looking, or they play in places that should remain quiet and sacred.	The gaming community needs to regulate its use of Pokemon Go so that players stay safe and engaged with the real world while they enjoy their communities and their exercise. The app could have start/stop options to keep users safe.	Pokemon Go has been a boon to gamers across the globe since it helps formerly couch-bound gamers get out into society, form communities and get exercise.

ESSAY 20

Essay Task

Write a unified, coherent essay about Pokemon Go. In your essay, be sure to::

- Clearly state your own perspective on the issue and analyze the relationship between your perspective and at least one other perspective
- Develop and support your ideas with reasoning and examples
- Organize your ideas clearly and logically
- Communicate your ideas effectively in standard written English

Your perspective may be in full agreement with any of those given, in partial agreement or completely different.

Planning sheets and Answer sheets can be downloaded from
the **Online Resource** section of this book on
www.vibrantpublishers.com

ESSAY 20

This page is intentionally left blank.

II

Solutions

Essay 3
Free-Range Kids – Who Decides?

Children learn and grow at different times and at different levels. Sometimes what is right for one kid is not right for another. Some children are ready to go off and "fly" at an early age while others take a little longer to leave the nest. The question is who gets to make the final choice about when the kids are ready. Parents should be able to decide whether or not to send their children off to a friend's house or an activity under their own steam if they deem the child's maturity level high enough to handle the moves, and it is not the community's or the police force's job to make that decision for the parents.

Introduction and thesis statement

Most often, parents know their child best and should be able to assess his or her maturity level. In most families, parents know their kids pretty well. They know if the child makes good decisions, such as doing homework before playing video games or choosing to spend time with friends who are good people as well as fun to be around. The parents who do things like have dinner with their children or at least speak to them after school about what is happening in their lives can often make a good assessment of their kid's ability to be mature and take responsibility for himself or herself. One similar situation is when kids fly by themselves on airplanes. Different airlines set the age at which kids can fly as unaccompanied minors but the parents have to take responsibility to know when their child can handle the "alone-ness" that comes with flying solo. Parents and children together can decide what is the right course of action.

Supporting Paragraph: Example I

The idea of kids on their own leads to the notion that parents have the right to allow their appropriately mature child to be "free-range" and travel around town locally on their own steam, or they can decide to accompany their child to and from various events and activities. Some parents prefer to be at their child's side all the time and some parents want to give their children responsibility for getting places on their own. Neither way is right; it depends on what the family decides. There was a case in Silver Spring Maryland where two kids, brother and sister, were walking from their home to the local library less than a mile away. Police saw them and took them into custody. A protracted investigation involving child protective services occurred to make sure that the parents were not neglecting their children. In the end, the parents were cleared of wrongdoing, but it definitely gave everyone a scare. Parents should have the right to make decisions for their children, which that case proves.

Supporting Paragraph: More examples

Like in the prior example, some people believe that local law enforcement and community leaders should fully protect children, Police forces, community activists and child protective services should take care before stepping in to

Counter Argument with examples

Solutions

accuse parents of neglect when those parents have made the conscious decision about the ability of their children to move around safely. The parents in the example had to prove that they had faith in their children; that their children were fully accustomed to walking to the library; that the children knew the route and the time and all sorts of other details; and that the children indeed wanted to be alone to go to the library. It was a long process when in fact, the police should have just left the children alone. If something is amiss then it is good to say something and ferret out trouble, but when two kids are innocently walking to the library, it would be better if they were left alone by the authorities.

Parents know their kids and most often, astute kids know their limits. In most cases the children would speak up if they felt uncomfortable doing something their parents ask them to do. There is always an exception to the rule, but in general, the authorities should leave it to the parents to decide on how and when to give their children autonomy.

Conclusion

Essay 4
Incentives for Charitable Donations

People who listen to public radio know the power of giving AND receiving. When the radio stations have their twice-yearly membership drives, there are always thank you gifts available for the different giving levels. Giving donors and volunteers gifts in return for their charitable donations is a great idea because people enjoy "swag" and it brings people into the organization so they can further the mission of the organization effectively."

Introduction and thesis statement

All charities need donations of time and money and incentives are a great way to bring more people into the pool of donors. Sometimes charities hold gala balls to entice donors to hear more about the philanthropic work they do and the attendees cover the cost of the ticket to the ball. People who attend such events know that they are expected to donate further to the charity while they are there, and most often there are small trinkets of thanks available to the donors. Donors take home the trinket, and later they are able to see it and remember how great they felt that evening, perhaps spurring them on to make further donations if they are able. Incentives such as small trinkets make donors want to continue to donate.

Supporting Paragraph: Example I

Even at an event like a Gala, the gifts charities give their donors and volunteers are small, like t-shirts and mugs, and do not greatly affect the bottom line of the charity; most of the money still goes to the mission of the organization. Even when a group of students goes on a mission trip to help build houses or teach children, most often the group gets a t-shirt from the charity that organizes the trip. It reminds the participants of the joy that suffused them when they saw the meaningful work they did come to fruition in the joy of the recipients. Charity is just as much for the donor as it is for the recipient and the small gifts the charity can give those donors or volunteers does not cost too much and means so much to the donor.

Supporting Paragraph: More examples

Sometimes the trinkets or t-shirts are unwanted by the donors, so while the gifts given by the charities by way of saying thank you are small, if people do not like the idea of an incentive gift, and they want to refuse the gift, then they are more than welcome to do so if their motivation is not affected by the gift. Some people are internally motivated and do not need the gift or shirt as a reminder of how good they felt when giving of their time or money. They do not want the charity to spend even a penny of that donated money on a gift for donors. That is completely fine and those people are free to refuse the gift. It does not change the fact that some people like to get a small gift and are motivated by it to continue to donate.

Counter Argument with examples

Solutions

Incentives to donate to charity or volunteer time on behalf of a charitable organization are small ways that the charity can say thank you and they might even serve to motivate continued donation and volunteerism. It is a win-win situation.

Conclusion

Solutions

Essay 5
Regulating the Size of Sugary Drinks

OUTLINE

Counter argument topic sentence

While the limiting of sugary drinks might help obesity rates, many people believe that having a government entity tell people what to eat or drink is too severe of a limit on freedom.

Regulating the Size of Sugary Drinks

Stores and restaurants make it very easy to super-size drinks in the U.S. If a medium sized drink is $1, then a large is often only $1.50. People don't mind spending an extra fifty cents to get a lot more drink, which means that most often people buy the large size of soda or juice from a fountain. The byproduct of the large drink is a large amount of sugar from the drinks going right into people's diet. In 2015 in New York City, the mayor tried to pass an ordinance that would forbid the sale of drinks over 16 ounces, but many people fought against the ordinance. However, the government of the City of New York should be able to limit the size of all sugary drinks available to the public in order to reduce citizens' sugar intake and ultimately the overall obesity rate in the city, which will ultimately reduce health care costs overall."

Introduction and thesis statement

The main reason the idea of size limit is important is because if the city government can limit the size of drinks available then people will buy fewer drinks that contain large amounts of sugar, which will lower their sugar intake considerably. The average American takes in at least three times the amount of sugar that is recommended by the Food and Drug Administration. Sugar is found in all types of processed food but is very prevalent in all types of sodas and juices. The larger the drink, the more sugar people get into their systems. If the drinks were required to be smaller, like a more reasonable twelve ounces instead of twenty or more, then people would necessarily absorb less sugar.

Supporting Paragraph: Example 1

If people are able to lower their sugar intake, then they will lower their chances of becoming obese, so ultimately the sugar limit could lower those obesity rates city-wide. Increased sugar intake is one of the biggest causes of obesity. People often do not realize how much sugar they have in every meal. They might not realize how many grams of sugar is in one of those drinks they consume every day. Often juices are labeled as "natural" or with a certain percentage of real fruit juice. The

Supporting Paragraph: More examples

rest of the sweetness in the drinks comes from a sugar derivative such as corn syrup or sucralose. The calories creep up slowly but surely and people find themselves gaining weight without realizing where the calories come from. This cascading domino effect might be prevented if at least the drinks people consume in the city were smaller. In that way, the smaller drinks would lower sugar intake, which in turn would lower obesity rates, a different type of good domino effect.

While the limiting of sugary drinks might help obesity rates, many people believe that having a government entity tell people what to eat or drink is too severe of a limit on freedom. People often feel that the government should not impede their right to make choices of any type. People do not want the city of New York to regulate how much sugar they can ingest and they might think that becoming overweight is their free choice. They might not want to think about where the calories come from or what harm they are doing to their bodies with the extra calories and extra weight. However, what people also to not understand is the impact the rising obesity rates have on the rest of the public. Higher obesity rates mean higher healthcare costs and that spills over to the general public, not just affecting the person in question but also society in general.

Counter Argument with examples

The City of New York tried to address the problem of rising obesity rates in the city in a small way by limiting the size of sugary drinks available to purchase. The mayor truly believed that he could address the rising obesity problem and thus rising healthcare costs in this small way, but ultimately people felt that their freedom was more important than the rising healthcare costs caused by the rising obesity rates and the measure did not pass. The important part in this case is that they tried and they did succeed in raising a little bit of awareness. The people who care will continue to address the problem and fight on.

Conclusion

Solutions

Essay 6
Golf: Sport or Game?

OUTLINE

Topic sentence (More examples)

Golfers burn a third of what soccer players and lacrosse players burn over a one-hour time period.

Counter argument topic sentence

Though some people consider golf a sport because it takes considerable skill and talent to be successful, there are many games including darts and table tennis that also require skill and talent and they are not sports.

Alternative counter argument to reach into the financial: Just because Nike and Adidas have paid millions of dollars in endorsements to professional golfers does not mean that golf is a sport; rather it means that people are interested in watching anyone who is dynamic play a game well.

Golf: Sport or Game?

Hundreds of thousands of people go out every weekend to play a round of golf on a nearby course, enjoying the sun on their faces and sometimes a drink in their hands. In addition, every year millions of people sit in their homes to watch major golf tournaments such as the U.S. Open and the Masters on TV. While golf is fun and interesting to both play and watch, since it does not require a strong sense of athleticism, it is not technically a sport.

Introduction and thesis statement

Golfers can come in all shapes and sizes, tall and short, fat and thin, unlike in other sports. Basketball players and soccer players are among the most fit people in the world. They are tall and thin and they work out almost every day, so not only are they fit, but they are fitness-minded. It takes a strong will to get into the shape needed to play most sports. The best basketball players in the world such as Kobe Bryant or LeBron James spend hours and hours in athletic training every single day. They spend more hours on the court throwing free-throw after free-throw to ensure that when they are called up to that line in a real game, they do not miss. In contrast, golfers need to swing a club every day and they need to get onto the links on a regular basis weekly, but they do not spend hours a day in a gym running or lifting weights. While a higher fitness level might give some golfers an edge, the hours spent training do not correlate to a better game like in other sports,

Supporting Paragraph: Example 1

Solutions

which makes golf a game, not a sport.

Furthermore, Golfers burn a third of what soccer players and lacrosse players burn over a one-hour time period. Walking a golf course while playing does not require the physical exertion of being on a soccer pitch or lacrosse field. Lacrosse players regularly run from one end of the field to the other. They bob and weave through the traffic of other players to get to their goal. All of that movement takes constant energy. In golf the players take a swing, then walk to the ball placement where they wait to take their next swing. It is true that golf courses are long and take time to traverse, but it does not take a lot of energy or burn a lot of calories to play a round of golf. Therefore the lack of energy expenditure means that golf is a game, not a sport.

Supporting Paragraph: More examples

Just because iconic sports-focused companies like Nike and Adidas have paid millions of dollars in endorsements to professional golfers does not mean that golf is a sport; rather it means that people are interested in watching anyone who is dynamic play a game well. Tiger Woods is not the first golfer to make money in endorsements, but rather he is the golfer that has made the most money with those endorsements. Tiger's entry into the world of golf in the late 1990's brought attention to golf in unprecedented numbers. All of a sudden people who had never looked at golf were finding it and watching it on TV in order to see his game. Even today when Tiger is not doing as well as in the past, people enjoy watching Tiger Woods play just because of the Cinderella story surrounding him. It made sense for the athletic apparel companies to capitalize on that sense of wonder by using Tiger in their advertisements. The sense of wonder spread to other golfers and soon there were large amounts of revenue available for golfers to star in ads for major athletic companies. However, advertisements and or even solid ratings do not mean that golf is a sport. Even with the million dollars of ad revenue golfers may receive, golf remains a game, like chess is a game and darts is a game, though both are shown on sports TV channels.

Counter Argument with examples

Golf is a wonderful way to spend a day and do a lot of walking. It's a great game to play as spring arrives and as fall fades into winter due to its outdoor focus. It is fun to watch the skill of the players on TV. However, golf is now and will remain a game, not a sport.

Conclusion

Essay 7
"Sin" Taxes

OUTLINE

Topic sentence (Example 1)

Excise taxes as high as $1 per pack on cigarettes or $1 per liter of alcohol will make people think twice about buying those items and the rates of smoking and alcoholism will lower.

Topic sentence (More examples)

If people do choose to buy cigarettes or alcohol, the money raised from the taxes could go to social programs such as welfare or early childhood education.

Counter argument topic sentence

The main problem with taxing some items and not others is that the decisions of which items to tax is in the hands of only a few people, but they are elected officials, so the public will have to trust them to do what is right for their constituents.

"Sin" Taxes

People will always engage in risky or socially unacceptable behavior, from smoking cigarettes to abusing alcohol. Some people believe that if those behaviors were more expensive then the high cost would dissuade people from partaking, so state and federal governments have tried to impose excise taxes on certain items that lead to morally questionable activities. Taxes on commodities such as gambling, smoking or even sugary drinks make sense because they might dissuade usage and the tax will also help pay for relevant social programs in the U.S."

Introduction and thesis statement

Excise taxes as high as $1 per pack on cigarettes or $1 per liter of alcohol will make people think twice about buying those items and the rates of smoking and alcoholism might lower. The number of people who smoke continues to lower and the numbers of people starting to use cigarettes, including teens, lowers yearly. Some of that is because of the public nature of the health issues caused by smoking, but some of it is due to the rising taxes that many jurisdictions have placed on the cigarettes themselves. To date there have been fewer taxes on alcohol and none on sugary drinks, both of which can cause serious health problems, but if those items were taxed at the same rate as cigarettes perhaps people would purchase them in smaller qualities and abuse them less. If fewer

Supporting Paragraph: Example 1

people abused alcohol and sugar, then the associated health care costs might lower. Setting a flat tax on so-called sinful items makes sense to dissuade people from engaging in morally questionable behavior.

In addition, if people do choose to buy cigarettes or alcohol, the money raised from the taxes could go to social programs such as welfare or early childhood education. It might be easy for people to obtain cigarettes and alcohol if they are a certain age, and there is currently no limit on the amount of soda and juice people can purchase, so if there was a flat tax those items, it would be easy to collect and the money could go toward interesting and helpful social programs. Imagine if every dollar people make at a casino from gambling was taxed for a few pennies. Those few pennies would add up and the coffers would fill, allowing governments to invest in social programs like early childhood education, which has a reputation for underpaying teachers of our most important resource: the youngest children. It might make sense for each jurisdiction to decide for themselves which items get taxed and which do not and have the Federal government stay out of the process. For example, not every state has casinos but those that do should be able to decide which programs to fund. Some areas do not have problems with people and sugary drinks, but some places that have more tourists than others would make money from charging visitors who buy sugary drinks instead of water. In that way, local and/or state governments could make the necessary decisions instead of leaving it to the Federal government, which might not make the right choice for every locality.

Supporting Paragraph: More examples

The main problem with taxing some items and not others is that the decisions of which items to tax is in the hands of only a few people, but they are elected officials, so the public will have to trust them to do what is right for their constituents. In 2015 in New York City, the Mayor decided to try to limit the amount of soda that could be in a restaurant or vendor's single serving in order to prevent so much sugar intake of residents and visitors alike, but in the end, people did not want any type of government telling them what to drink and how much of it. Freedom was more important to them. If politicians try to levy an excise tax on so-called "sinful" items like alcohol and gambling, then they essentially function as morality police to tell people what is good behavior and what is not. So that type of decision on good vs. evil is left in the hands of a few politicians in certain localities. There are many people who will not like being told what to do and when and how. That being said, the politicians should be able to campaign on the idea of raising money for social programs via these taxes, and perhaps more of their constituents would join the bandwagon and allow the taxes to go through. It is up to the politicians to win the hearts of the people in order to impose taxes, and ultimately the benefit of the taxes outweighs the negative aspects.

Counter Argument with examples

Solutions

People will always take part in risky behaviors but if local governments can capitalize on that proclivity then they might be able to fill state coffers and lower the number of people engaging in those behaviors. Sometimes a little taxing is a good idea.

Conclusion

Essay 8
Advertising Prescription Drugs

Thesis statement

"The FDA should strengthen their regulations on advertising prescription drugs directly to consumers so that potential patients get the correct information about treatments and take medication the right way."

OUTLINE

Topic sentence (Example 1)

Even though the timing is not ideal, allowing the FDA to regulate advertising directly to consumers ensures correct information is transmitted regarding the treatment of the illness and application of the drug.

Topic sentence (More examples)

The regulation of advertisements by the FDA ensures safety of information so more people can purchase the drugs and the drug companies can spend more money on medical research for new treatments of different illnesses.

Counter argument topic sentence

Advertising prescription drugs directly to consumers might put pressure on healthcare providers, who then might over-prescribe them, but ultimately the doctors should do what they feel is right for the individual patient presenting the request.

Advertising Prescription Drugs

It happens on a daily basis: you're watching a TV show and there's a commercial break. All of sudden on the screen appears a person with a serious illness telling you that he or she has been cured via a certain medication and the viewer is exhorted to speak to his or her doctor. Then the announcer lists the potential side effects of the medication so quickly you're left breathless and wondering why anyone would take the drug in the first place. Advertising prescription drugs directly to consumers is a relatively new phenomenon and it is controversial. There are very few countries across the globe where people can see advertisements for prescription drugs on television. To be as safe as possible, the FDA should strengthen their regulations on advertising prescription drugs directly to consumers so that potential patients get the correct information about treatments and take medication the right way.

Even though the timing is not ideal, allowing the FDA to regulate advertising

Introduction and thesis statement

directly to consumers ensures correct information is transmitted regarding the treatment of the illness and application of the drug. The FDA does not see advertisements for prescription medication before they are released to the public; they only see the ads after they have been in the market for a little while, which means that if the ad has already been transmitted to the public, whether it is giving correct information or not. However, bad timing for regulation is better than no regulation at all. The FDA officials do get to see and analyze the advertisements to ensure that all of the information listed within is exactly correct. The ads actually ensure that the consumer has all of the information they might want about a given treatment for various diseases. Patients can learn about the way the medication works, as well as the medication's potential side effects all within a space of thirty seconds. The ads clear the FDA and the consumers know they can trust the information they're given.

Supporting Paragraph: Example 1

It is specifically the trust of the consumer underlying the FDA's regulation of advertisements that encourages people to purchase the drugs, so then the drug companies can spend more money on medical research for new treatments of different illnesses. Globally American drug companies spend more money on research for new treatments than companies in any other country. Americans are the leader in research and the rest of the world relies on that research. It is no wonder that the U.S. is one of two countries in the world that allows direct-to-consumer advertising, the other being New Zealand. If the drug companies do not have the funds for research, then new treatments for various diseases will take significantly longer to come to market, so more people will not be treated. The advertising directly contributes to consumers discussing treatment options with their physicians and making the decision to try various drug regimens. The drug companies have the opportunity to reinvest those profits into research. The regulation of the advertising makes consumers feel safe in making the purchase, thus indirectly contributing to research.

Supporting Paragraph: More examples

Safety is always a concern and some people feel that advertising prescription drugs directly to consumers might put pressure on healthcare providers, who then might over-prescribe them, but ultimately the doctors should do what they feel is right for the individual patient presenting the request. Whether or not patients see an advertisement for their illness and its treatment or not, it still behooves doctors to know their patients and prescribe the exact right drug and dosage for each individual, so the ads should not make a difference in that regard. Both the doctor and the patient together must decide on a treatment plan, so whether or not the drugs are advertised on TV should be irrelevant to the conversation. Safety is the priority of the FDA, as well as doctors globally.

Counter Argument with examples

Currently people see advertisements for prescription drugs on a regular basis. Regardless of the drug, it is incumbent upon doctors and patients to design a plan of treatment that contains the correct drugs and dosages, and no amount of advertising will should make a difference when discussing patient health. The FDA should continue to regulate the advertisements for prescription drugs to ensure safety and correct dissemination of information for everyone.

Conclusion

Solutions

Essay 9
Buying Bottled Water

DECONSTRUCT THE ARGUMENT

Pros-

3. If more people use refillable water bottles, then there will be less debris left on the streets after big events in parks and cities (think parades or carnivals).

4. Lowering the amount of plastics used helps the environment with landfill use and recycling costs.

Cons-

3. If bottled water is not available then people will buy what IS available, including soda and juice, which contribute to the U.S. obesity problems.

Thesis statement

"The ability to buy individual bottles of water at large public events is important to the people attending and to limit the sale would effectively put limits on the personal freedom of people in those situations."

OUTLINE

Topic sentence (Example 1)

At various public events like concerts and parades and sporting events, many small vendors fulfill the hydration needs of attendees by selling individual-sized bottles of water, and the inability to do so would hurt those businesses.

Topic sentence (More examples)

Similarly, if people attending large, public events cannot buy individually sized bottles of water then there is effectively a limit placed on their personal freedom.

Counter argument topic sentence

It is much less expensive to buy a refillable water bottle and carry it everywhere but often there is not a place to fill it and people will end up buying juice or soda which is not as hydrating and puts extra sugar into people which might contribute to the American obesity problem.

Buying Bottled Water

It has happened to everyone: you've been outside all day and become thirsty. You need to buy a bottle of water. Some cities in the U.S. are considering a ban on buying individual water bottles at large, public events citing the environmental harm from the plastic bottles, and encouraging people to bring refillable bottles instead. However, the ability to buy individual bottles of water at large public events is important to the people attending and to limit the sale would effectively put limits on the personal freedom of people in those situations."

Introduction and thesis statement

At various public events like concerts and parades and sporting events, many small vendors fulfill the hydration needs of attendees by selling individual-sized bottles of water, and the inability to do so would hurt those businesses. The lines for food and drink generally wind around the corner at arenas and other venues because people demand hydration, and most often just want water, not other drinks. Sometimes the vendors inside the arenas or in parks are contractors and their small companies contract with the park or arena to be able to sell their wares at the event. If people cannot buy water bottles and instead, have to carry refillable water bottles to fill at filling stations, then the small company, which is not allowed to sell the water, will go out of business. The lines at the bottle-filling stations will become unbearable, even worse than the lines to purchase food since at the purchase lines, vendors are able to fulfill a need and move people through as quickly as possible. The filling stations for bottles will likely not be manned. In addition, the inability to have vendors sell water bottles is a revenue loss for the arena or park because the vendors sometimes pay a flat fee but sometimes pay a percentage of sales to the park or vendor. The idea of preventing water bottle sales is an all-around money loser.

Supporting Paragraph: Example 1

Similarly, if people attending large, public events cannot buy individually sized bottles of water then there is effectively a limit placed on their personal freedom. People should be able to purchase and eat or drink exactly what they prefer at that moment and if they want a bottle of water they should be able to purchase it. If vendors are not allowed to sell water because it is available at filling stations, then people will resort to drinking things besides water, which might not be their first preference; their freedom to buy what they wanted was eliminated. If local officials start legislating what people can eat or drink, in what form and how much, then it is a slippery slope to the limit of individuals to have freedom over what they do or do not put into their bodies. Limiting the sale of bottled water can start that slide.

Supporting Paragraph: More examples

Granted, it is much less expensive to buy a refillable water bottle and carry it everywhere but often there is not a place to fill it and people will end up buying juice or soda which is not as hydrating and puts extra sugar into people which might contribute to the American obesity problem. Patrons at large parks and arenas where events are taking place are there to see a band, play with kids or generally have a good time. They should not have to think about where their

Counter Argument with examples

water might come from. Some people already do carry refillable water bottles and are willing to spend time looking for the stations at which to fill them. There are still plenty of people who are not willing to carry and fill and those people will look for alternatives. If they cannot buy bottles of water, they will resort to buying bottles of soda or juice, which still have plastic that is not good for the environment, but now they will be consuming extra sugar or chemicals that will only increase their odds for becoming obese, staring yet another problem. The simplest solution will be to allow vendors to continue selling water.

Limiting vendors' ability to sell water at large, public events is a limit on everyone's personal freedom, both the vendor and the purchaser. It is a financial strain as well as a potential contributor to the American obesity problem. Vendors should be able to sell water whenever and wherever they choose in order to hydrate the patrons.

Conclusion

Solutions

Essay 10
A Computer for Every Student

DECONSTRUCT THE ARGUMENT

Pros-

2. The 1:1 ratio allows for better teaching of concepts such as digital citizenship and responsible use.

3. The 1:1 ratio aspect allows for equity in the classes; there will not be some wealthy students with fancy computers and some less advantaged students without any machines; everyone will have the same tools.

Cons-

2. Studies show that students who work on public computers vs. private computers do not necessarily have better learning outcomes.

3. Students are not going to take good care of the machines and they will have to be replaced often due to maintenance needs.

Thesis statement

"Programs in public schools in the U.S. that give all students their own computer help students become better digital citizens, promote equity in the classroom and prepare the students for college and beyond, but require dedicated maintenance staff and buy-in from faculty in order to succeed."

OUTLINE

Topic sentence (Example 1)

If each student has his or her own computer in the classroom, it will promote equity and boost confidence of otherwise disadvantaged students.

Topic sentence (More examples)

Having an individual computer helps students learn digital citizenship, collaboration skills, and other skills they might need in college and beyond.

Counter argument topic sentence

While the idea of having a computer for every student is a great idea, it can only be successful if there are clearly enumerated learning goals, and dedicated staff to maintain the machines, as well as faculty buy-in.

A Computer for Every Student

Students need to be computer savvy in order to survive not only in school, but also in college, in the workplace and beyond. School districts need to prepare students for the collaborative environment of today's world. Each student learns at a different rate so sometimes sharing machines in classrooms does not work well. Sometimes one computer for every student should be the goal for all schools, but in particular grades 9-12 where students are preparing for life beyond high school. Programs in public schools in the U.S. that give all students their own computer help students become better digital citizens, promote equity in the classroom and prepare the students for college and beyond, but require dedicated maintenance staff and buy-in from faculty in order to succeed.

Introduction and thesis statement

If each student has his or her own computer in the classroom, it will promote equity and boost confidence of otherwise disadvantaged students. Even in communities where the more privileged students each have their own laptop, often students with fewer resources at home share one computer among all family members or use a public computer at a library or other location for homework or other important schoolwork. If school districts provided every student with a laptop or other personal device for use during the school year, then it might erase, or at least ease, some differences between students. Having a personal computer might go a long way in making less privileged students feel like they have the implements they need to do the work; it might even help them feel more like they can do better work – work more successfully – with the proper tools. A computer for every student has great potential to help all students feel strong.

Supporting Paragraph: Example I

In addition to feeling strong and successful, having an individual computer helps students learn digital citizenship, collaboration skills, and other skills they might need in college and beyond. If the schools are committed to having the 1:1 computer programs then they will need ways to help students learn to use the machines. In addition to the simple technology classes, the students will use the computer as a tool in their academic classes. They will be able to collaborate and do group work much more easily in any class, given the tools and software accessible on current computers. In addition, in a safe environment, students will learn digital citizenship. They will learn proper behavior online, in groups, and when communicating on social media. Lessons on these topics and others will be included in academic classes like English and history and be tied to the areas of study. Media studies will be easier when students can each look up their own ideas of proper publications to be studying instead of only doing group work around one machine. These are skills that students will recall and rely on for the rest of their academic careers and beyond – all starting based on the 1:1 computer

Supporting Paragraph: More examples

Solutions

program.

The students definitely need to learn the skills of the future such as digital citizenship and the idea of having a computer for every student is a great idea, but it can only be successful if there are clearly enumerated learning goals, and dedicated staff to maintain the machines, as well as faculty buy-in. Technology for technology's sake never works and is never appropriately utilized. When starting a 1:1 computer program, schools must make a conscious decision HOW they are going to use the machines. They need to hire appropriate staff to teach the technology and the soft skills that the students need to take advantage of the big investment. They have to have proper maintenance staff as well – the computers break down and students are hard on the machines. The computers will need some care on a regular basis. All this means that the investment goes well beyond the initial investment in the machines themselves. The investment extends to teaching and maintenance staff. And lastly, unless the teachers understand the value of the investment, it will never be properly utilized. The teachers are the life-blood of the system. If they do not enthusiastically embrace the program and commit to using the machines in class then the entire program will not work. The teachers are the ones who have the most contact and influence with the students; the teachers' attitudes will be the success of the program. Many factors must be in place to have a successful implementation of 1:1 computer programs.

Counter Argument with examples

All in all, if school districts implement a 1:1 computer program, it will boost student confidence, prepare students for life beyond secondary school and then hopefully have good results for learning overall. The investment is high, but the potential success factors outweigh the negatives.

Conclusion

Essay 11
School Uniforms

DECONSTRUCT THE ARGUMENT

Pros-

1. Uniforms promote unity within the school.

2. Uniforms erase class difference between students.

3. Uniforms rather than just a dress code takes less time for administrators to "police" due to the clarity of the outward evidence.

4. Uniforms can improve punctuality since students don't spend time worrying about what to wear.

5. Uniforms keep students safe since they cannot show gang affiliations or other insignias.

Cons-

1. School uniforms restrict the personal freedom of students and promote conformity instead of individuality.

2. Uniforms have to be purchased, which undermines the idea of a free public education.

3. In addition, uniforms get faded and tattered just as much as regular clothing so replacing uniforms is an added expense.

4. Uniforms restrict parents' right to choose what their children wear as well.

5. Students themselves usually do not want to wear uniforms.

Thesis statement

"Students in public schools should not have to wear uniforms to class because of the restrictions it puts on the freedoms of both students and parents to make choices and even if the school does choose a uniform policy, there is not a guarantee that it will fulfill all of the promises uniforms purport."

OUTLINE

Topic sentence (Example 1)

School uniforms restrict the creative and expressive freedoms of students of every age.

Solutions

Topic sentence (More examples)

School uniforms undermine the ability of parents to choose what their children wear and the students generally do not want to wear them, causing chaos at home.

Counter argument topic sentence

Even though school uniforms might mitigate class differences in the beginning, the uniforms get faded and tattered as much as every other article of clothing so after some wear and tear, they need replacing, which is easier for some parents to do than others, which only exacerbates class difference.

School Uniforms

Burning an American flag. Yelling "fire" in a crowded movie theater. Shouting racial slurs at minority groups. Since its founding, America has been rocked with scandals and incidents related to one of the most significant rights expressed in the Bill of Rights, the right to free speech and expression. To what extent can authorities limit free speech to help society as a whole? This issue has evolved through the years and is now especially prevalent within American schools. Students and parents are particularly concerned with the new dress codes and school uniforms being imposed at schools. In 2015, 21% of public schools in America had a school uniform, and the number has grown since. Public school districts in the United States should require students to wear some sort of uniform, as it provides a sense of unity and a multitude of related academic benefits.

Introduction and thesis statement

School districts should impose a school uniform on students as it ensures that students can stay focused in all academic settings. Students across the country suffer from learning disabilities from ADHD to hyperactivity, and every distraction in a classroom can be the difference between a good and bad grade in a class. Additionally, students in schools without strict school uniforms often come to school with purposely offensive clothing, from political slogans to ads for drinking. These pieces of clothing often draw students' eyes away from the lesson and teacher and to the student wearing them. If the students are even mildly distracted in class, they will miss material covered on exams. However, if a school imposes a school uniform on all students, the distraction of different clothing and styles will be removed from the classroom. With the school uniform, students cannot wear offensive clothing, or even different colors of clothing. This ensures that students will pay attention to the only different object in the room- the board and the teacher. Thus, school districts should impose a school uniform on all students to promote focus and a sense of unity.

Supporting Paragraph: Example 1

In America, school districts should impose a school uniform on students to decrease the perceived stratification of their students. In school, a sensitive topic for every student is their socioeconomic status relative to other students in the school. Clothing is often a significant sign of status—higher-class students with

Supporting Paragraph: More examples

large resources will wear designer clothing and custom shoes, while lower class students will wear thrift store clothing or hand me downs. This difference, this split, only exasperated tensions within the school. In schools without school uniforms, students who cannot afford expensive clothing may feel ashamed or even bullied by other students. However, if a school imposes a school uniform on students, this perceived difference in status will disappear. Students will no longer feel the need to struggle past their resources to fit in and dress like other students. The school uniform code provides a blank slate for lower income students to reinvent themselves, pushing past prejudice based on their background, and focusing on academic pursuits. Thus, school districts should impose a school uniform on all students to decrease stratification, establish a sense of unity, and create academic progress.

Lastly, schools should impose a school dress code on their students as it promotes a sense of unity amongst students. One of my friends attends a local Catholic high school, and while she commiserates with her peers and others on the uniform she is forced to wear, she is united with her peers within the uniform. Under the school dress code, every student wears the same thing, and the uniform becomes an expression of school spirit. Students who had nothing in common before now have a bridge to connect to other students. Bullying over socioeconomic status will decrease, and lower-class students will no longer feel ashamed to attend school. In turn, this creates a beneficial atmosphere in school and an end to reluctance to attend school. School spirit rises, and with it, happiness and academic achievement. Thus, school districts should impose a school uniform on all students to increase unity, school spirit, and academic progress.

However, another perspective on this issue is that school uniforms violate the freedom of expression rights of students. Those who hold this view say the United States Bill of Rights protects students' right to wear whatever they wish. But this view is simply not true and violates the rights of many students. The court system in America has repeatedly established that freedom of expression is not protected in schools, as administrators must have the ability to enforce dress codes to limit distractions and dangers within schools. Additionally, the right to free expression in school violates the right to a detailed education of many low-income students. The lack of a school uniform makes these students feel lower and distracts many other students from an unobstructed learning environment.

Counter Argument with examples

In America, there is a debate over affirmative action, institutional bias, and the benefits of equality v/s equity. We must choose equity to help those who have been pushed down again and again in this country. School districts must impose a school uniform on all students, as the school uniform is a relatively easy way to create blank slates for all students, slates on which beneficial educations can be built. America must be the leader in taking steps to address the deep inequality in worldwide education.

Conclusion

Solutions

Essay 12
Free Tuition at State Universities

DECONSTRUCT THE ARGUMENT

Pros-

Students should not have to pay tuition for their state schools to give them a good education.

1. Free tuition will solve the problem of the crippling student loan debts in the U.S.

2. As the job market has changed, so has the nature of work so students need a university degree to get a good job. Most of the in-demand jobs require the degree and as such, everyone deserves a university education, regardless of their ability to pay.

3. In the past, things like the GI bill sent people to college for free so there is a precedent for tuition-free state universities.

Cons-

1. Giving free tuition to state universities will cause states to have astronomical tax rates so that it will be hard to live in those states.

2. Paying for someone to attend college does not mean guaranteeing a degree. Some students begin and never finish due to lack of perseverance, lack of continued funding beyond tuition or lack of ability to handle the workload.

3. Students forget that the cost of room and board is high so they might still have to take loans to cover the cost, so paying for tuition doesn't completely eliminate debt.

Thesis statement

There is no doubt that every student deserves to be educated to the best of their ability or desire, but free tuition is not the answer to the problem of rising tuition rates at state universities because students might still take loans for room and board, they might start school and never finish, leaving only the room and board loans to be paid and similarly, students might still finish with student loan debts due to the crushing and ever-increasing costs of a university education.

OUTLINE

Topic sentence (Example 1)

The tax rate will become prohibitive if states try to subsidize tuition at universities because high taxes seems to be the only way to defray the costs of the tuition on the state.

Topic sentence (More examples)

There is still the cost of room and board, which can be quite expensive, to be considered, so some students will still have to take loans to make ends meet even if they do not pay the tuition part of the student bill.

Counter argument topic sentence

No one would argue that every person should have the right to work up to his or her potential, which might include a college degree, one that could be out of reach financially for a student, but simply giving the student free tuition does not solve the other assorted problems, including the high drop-out rate projected for students who receive the benefit.

Free Tuition at State Universities

A college education is a goal of many students but there are still millions of people a year who have to forgo college after their high school years due to the high costs associated with achieving higher education. There is no doubt that every student deserves to be educated to the best of their ability or desire, but free tuition is not the answer to the problem of raising attendance rates at state universities because students might still take loans for room and board, they might start and never finish, leaving only the room and board payments and similarly, they might still have student loan debts due to the crushing and ever-increasing and varied costs of an education.

Introduction and thesis statement

The tax rate will become prohibitive if states try to subsidize tuition at universities because high taxes seems to be the only way to defray the costs of the tuition on the state. Public institutions have a significant portion of their costs paid for by the state, and if tuition is free at state universities, then somehow the state has to recoup that money. The easiest and fastest way to raise money for a state is to increase the tax rate on all individuals, and perhaps more steeply on the richest people. Some places have tried other ways to increase revenue but they have not been as successful as raising taxes, which effects all residents of the state, not just those who have students who will benefit from the free tuition. Raising taxes

Supporting Paragraph: Example 1

Solutions

across the board in a state in order to offer free tuition is not an equitable solution

Even if tuition is free at state institutions, there is still the cost of room and board to consider, which can be quite expensive, so some students will still have to take loans to make ends meet even if they do not pay the tuition part of the student bill. Room and board costs include all of the students' living expenses and can equal quite a large amount, even at a state school. Residence halls can be more costly than apartments with roommates and most students who live in residence halls are required to have meal plans at the university, even small ones. Sometimes students can find less expensive living quarters with relatives or friends and consume lower cost food, but costs such as books and other fees will still remain beyond tuition. A free tuition bill would not cover these other assorted costs and students would still struggle, just in a different way. Some students would still have to take a loan to cover the other costs.

Supporting Paragraph: More examples

Beyond the cost consideration, no one would argue that every person should have the right to work up to his or her potential, which might include a college degree, one that could be out of reach financially for a student, but simply giving the student free tuition does not solve the other assorted problems, including the high drop-out rates and other problems. Some students will be able to handle the demands of college and some students will not. Offering free tuition does not mean that every student should go to college. What the U.S. really needs is options beyond college that are reasonably priced and just as respected. We need to have good options like high level, prestigious trade schools that prepare students beyond high school to work at jobs they enjoy and that could be quite lucrative as well. A college education should not be the only choice for post-secondary students, and indeed other options might have more equitable solutions.

Counter Argument with examples

It is often tempting for students to advocate for free college tuition from legislators before they understand all of the nuanced issues associated with the plan. Free tuition does not mean a completely free education and it is not equitable for everyone in the state. Trade schools might be an excellent option for some students and their prestige should be raised. All in all, the rising costs of a university education must be addressed, but forcing states to pay so much for it is not the right solution

Conclusion

Essay 13
Honor Codes

DECONSTRUCT THE ARGUMENT

Pros-

Honor codes and the sanctions imposed for violation of the codes by Honor Councils, work to prevent further violation.

1. Honor codes are outlined in a student handbook for every student to clearly see so students should know what they are getting into if they make the choice to violate that code.

2. Sanctions such as failing the assignment in question or for stronger violations, failing the course, prove to be strong deterrents for academic dishonesty.

3. Honor codes cover more than just academics; places with a strong honor code make students feel safe and like they can walk around freely, unafraid of crime or harm.

Cons-

Honor code violations are either too harsh or too obscure to be effective deterrents to further academic dishonesty.

1. Some students commit academic dishonesty without knowing it; international students are often unclear on American emphasis on plagiarism and how important it is to the universities, so sometimes the violation is inadvertent and imposed sanctions are too harsh.

2. Students should be taught to work together, so preventing collaboration and bringing a violation to the honor board is often counter to current work culture.

3. Research is still unclear on whether or not harsh sanctions really do prevent the crime of plagiarism or other academic dishonesty.

Thesis statement

"Academic dishonesty is a serious problem at universities across the U.S. so the institutions must form honor councils and create a statement outlining violations and their consequences so students know what will happen if they commit such a breach, and then the fear of those consequences will prevent further misdeeds."

OUTLINE

Topic sentence (Example 1)

Academic dishonesty, including plagiarism is a violation of a school's honor code so the consequences must be harsh and imposed quickly to prevent violation.

Topic sentence (More examples)

If the consequences are hard enough then it is likely that other students will avoid committing academic dishonesty in fear of those consequences.

Counter argument topic sentence

Though swift and complete sanctions might prevent deliberate violations of honor codes, instances of violation must be taken on a case by case basis because sometimes the violation of an honor code might be inadvertent by someone who is not from the U.S. or simply does not understand the gravity of the problem, so in those cases justice can be meted out gently.

Honor Codes

Schools all over are finding that they have more and more cases of plagiarism and cheating across all disciplines in the university. The Internet makes cheating pretty simple, and students find the ability to take shortcuts very tempting, particularly if their school does not have a specific method of addressing such issues. Academic dishonesty is a serious problem at universities across the U.S. so the institutions must form honor councils and create statements outlining violations and their consequences so students know what will happen if they commit such a breach, and then the fear of those consequences will prevent further misdeeds.

Introduction and thesis statement

Academic dishonesty, including plagiarism should be a violation of a school's honor code so the consequences must be harsh and imposed quickly to prevent violation. Even if an honor code is somewhat "new" to the school like it is at Harvard (implemented in 2015) the professors and administrators must stay true to the spirit of the rule and ensure that all violators are punished accordingly. At many schools, the office of academic integrity will hold small hearings to let the students state their cases as to why they did not commit academic dishonesty if they believe they were falsely accused. Professors attend the hearings and give their side of the story as well and the board, which is most often comprised of students and professors together, gets to decide on the veracity of the students' cases and recommend sanctions. Sanctions can vary from assigning a failing grade to the assignment in question all the way to dismissal from the university for repeat offenders. Sometimes a student is deemed not guilty and the entire instance is expunged from the student's record, but that distinction is up to the

Supporting Paragraph: Example 1

Solutions

honor board to decide. Regardless, the hearings must occur as quickly as possible after the violation so that justice is meted out fairly and quickly and the student, if necessary, can recover his or her grade point average in the best way possible.

Supposing the hearings happen quickly, if the consequences are severe enough then it is likely that other students will avoid committing academic dishonesty in fear of those consequences. If a student is caught cheating on an exam in class, the penalty should be swift and severe so that other students notice what happened and can be warned to avoid the same actions. If students are caught plagiarizing on essays, it is particularly important to let them know and let the rest of the class understand how that behavior affects their grades. Plagiarism is a nuanced type of academic dishonesty and teachers must be sure that their students understand what it is and the severity of the associated penalties. Hopefully those actions will help students avoid the problems. The threat of swift and honest justice makes people avoid committing offenses in the first place.

Supporting Paragraph: More examples

Though swift and complete sanctions might prevent deliberate violations of honor codes, instances of violation must be taken on a case by case basis because sometimes the violation of an honor code might be inadvertent by someone who is not from the U.S. or simply does not understand the gravity of the problem, so in those cases justice can be meted out gently. Particularly with problems like plagiarism, international students might not have the idea of why such actions are problematic. Perhaps they are unaccustomed to working alone and might work with a partner, which would constitute cheating in certain cases. This is why honor boards are so important within the office of academic integrity. The honor board can hear cases individually and mete out sanctions if there is truly a crime committed. No one punishment fits all crimes, so not all sanctions are fit for every case of academic dishonesty.

Counter Argument with examples

Academic institutions of higher learning should have a strong office of academic integrity that allows students to have their cases heard before an honor board. In most of the cases, if the student is found guilty, then there should be swift and appropriate justice in the form of sanctions, some of which might be severe in the cases of repeat offenders. All of the work that goes into these honor boards will pay off in the way the sanctions and challenges will prevent others from copying the crimes in fear of the consequences. Then honor boards and offices of academic integrity will prove their value to the institution of higher learning.

Conclusion

Solutions

Essay 14
Arts Funding in Schools

ANALYSIS OF THE PROMPT

What is this prompt really asking?

There is more than just economics in this question. Students must consider the value of education in art, music and theater – not only to themselves but also to students across the spectrum of schools in the United States. What is it that the arts give to students and how can they capitalize on it? Does a music class count as a bit of "break" for students in their busy days? If education in the arts really does help raise test scores, then we owe it to students to continue the exposure. In areas where there is a low socioeconomic status, students might not have the opportunity to study music or art outside of the classroom so that perhaps we have a responsibility especially to students in those schools to fund arts education. One more area to consider is what might get cut from budgets instead of arts funding if there really does need to be a cut to make the school district run efficiently and debt-free.

DECONSTRUCT THE ARGUMENT

Pros-

Arts education should be funded in all schools in order to maintain optimal student performance.

1. Arts education has been shown to improve grades and test scores for students in low socioeconomic areas and in more privileged areas alike.

2. Arts education provides balance for students in their otherwise heavy, pressure-filled days.

3. Participation in music, visual art or theater increases college acceptance rates.

4. Participation in arts of any sort helps students create a community in their high schools.

5. Participation in the arts is a strong predictor of participation in other areas of high school life.

Cons-

There are many important programs to fund in schools and of course arts education is important, but other programs take priority.

1. Students' priority needs to be on "core" classes such as math, science,

English and History, so if a budget needs to be cut, non-mandatory classes such as those in the arts should be cut.

2. Students are tested on information in core classes, not arts classes, and in some cases, test score performance equates to continued/increased school funding so students must concentrate on those.

3. Students are more likely to use the information in their core classes later in life, so it makes sense to put the limited available funding into those classes, not arts classes.

Thesis statement

"When lawmakers look to cut school budgets, they often cite classes in art, music or theater as "expendable" but they might not understand all of the benefits students derive from classes in the arts, such as higher test scores, increased sense of community and better college acceptance rates, so arts classes should remain fully funded."

OUTLINE

Topic sentence (Example 1)

Studies have shown that when students take classes in the arts, such as music or visual art, they are more likely to succeed in other academic areas like math and science, thus raising test scores for the school in general, and making the school potentially eligible for more funding.

Topic sentence (More examples)

Further studies have noted that when students take classes in the arts, they find community with their peers and are then more likely to participate in other types of high school activities and communities such as athletics.

Counter argument topic sentence

Lawmakers who have to make choices about funding for schools cite core classes like history, math and science to be more important and more worthy of funding, but they often fail to see the connection between participation in the arts and success in those core classes.

Funding for Arts Programs

Balancing budgets for school systems is not ever an easy task. With costs for teacher salaries, supplies and other assorted staff rising every year, often lawmakers have to find room to make cuts and they have to be creative in how the money is spent or used. They try to find the places where students are least

Introduction and thesis statement

Solutions

effected both while in school and in the future. When lawmakers look to cut school budgets, they often cite classes in art, music or theater as "expendable" but they might not understand all of the benefits students derive from classes in the arts, such as higher test scores, increased sense of community and better college acceptance rates, so arts classes should remain fully funded.

Funding works in many ways and studies have shown that when students take classes in the arts, such as music or visual art, they are more likely to succeed in other academic areas like math and science, thus raising test scores for the school in general, and making the school potentially eligible for more funding. When enough students excel, the school districts can apply for more grants from both the State and Federal governments to fund special programs. One way to ensure that students excel in various subjects is to ask them to take classes in the arts. Higher math skills such as trigonometry and calculus are boosted by music; the ability to analyze literature is spurred by learning to draw. Funding classes in the arts is essential to success in other types of academics, and ultimately districts can apply to receive further funding.

Supporting Paragraph: Example 1

Just as importantly, further studies have noted that when students take classes in the arts, they find community with their peers and are then more likely to participate in other types of high school activities and communities such as athletics. For example, the numbers of students who participate in band or choir and also in a high school sport are astronomical. Students crave different types of communities and they look to various activities in high schools in which they can belong. Today's student does not want to be defined by just one activity so they look to their classes in art for one type of community and their sports for another. Community – a sense of belonging – is the highest predictor for stable mental health among teens. Without funding arts programs, schools will miss out on this important opportunity to help students find community and thus boost mental health.

Supporting Paragraph: More examples

Lawmakers who have to make choices about funding for schools cite core classes like history, math and science to be more important and more worthy of funding, but they often fail to see the connection between participation in the arts and success in those core classes. Study after study shows the correlation between learning to play an instrument and success in math class. Similar studies show the cognitive benefits of classes in visual arts. The lawmakers who are making decisions about funding see only the effects in the schools themselves and fail to see the effects on the students once they are done with school – if students have training in the arts, they will see further success in their core classes and achieve more in college and beyond. Not funding arts programs is short sighted even if it seems like the most expedient solution at the moment.

Counter Argument with examples

Running programs in the arts such as music, visual arts and theater might seem expensive in the short term, but students gain so much from participation in these programs that not funding them only hurts the children in the long run. Arts programs are crucial to the success of students in the U.S.

Conclusion

Solutions

Essay 15
Traditional Books vs. Reading Devices

ANALYSIS OF THE PROMPT

What is this prompt really asking?

This prompt is interesting because it gets at the future of education. Think about how you like best to read – or how you read best to achieve your learning goals. Sometimes the two ideas are in opposition because pleasure reading can be different than reading to learn. When reading to learn you must consider the factors of potential outside distractions, and the ways your brain processes information. On the surface, it might seem like tablets are the better option for students in terms of their ability to be updated and the sheer weight that students won't have to carry, but there are hefty upfront costs to tablets, and also costs to maintain them. It is up to you to make an argument for whichever side you deem most appropriate for the students of the future.

DECONSTRUCT THE ARGUMENT

Pros-

Tablets are a good investment for students in K-12 schools to help them stay current in their learning.

1. If they are given tablets for reading, students can update them whenever new versions of their textbooks are released.

2. Tablets are good for the environment because do they avoid printing books, but then teachers can send worksheets and other information to the tablet instead of printing and copying.

3. Students get physically weighed down with the heft of textbooks whereas carrying one tablet will significantly lighten the load.

4. Since tablets can be interactive, there is evidence that particularly with math, tablet use increases text scores.

Cons-

There is an abundance of evidence that students learn better with traditional textbooks than with tablets.

1. Students who use tablets in the classroom instead of traditional textbooks are significantly more distracted.

2. Studies show that reading is different on a tablet than a traditional textbook, less linear in nature, and that type of reading does not promote or facilitate deep thinking.

3. Tablet use requires a hefty up-front investment from the school and continued investment in updates and maintenance, which is much more costly than replacing textbooks.

4. Students can't use the excuse that their textbook crashed if they did not complete an assignment.

Thesis statement

"School districts should not invest in tablets for reading in the classroom because tablets prevent deep learning, promote distraction and the hefty upfront investment required is better spent on other programming."

OUTLINE

Topic sentence (Example 1)

Traditional textbooks can be read in a more linear fashion that promotes deeper learning than studies show happens with tablet reading and learning.

Topic sentence (More examples)

Traditional textbooks do not require the same hefty upfront costs as a tablet and require virtually no maintenance beyond tape.

Counter argument topic sentence

Though there is value in considering tablets for their ability to be updated and their low weight for student ease of carrying, ultimately students will learn better by using traditional textbooks.

Traditional Books vs. Reading Devices

As technology becomes ever more prevalent in classrooms, some schools are considering moving all of their reading matter to tablets in lieu of issuing students traditional books. There are pros and cons to having tablets, including issues of price and distraction, and often parents have particular opinions on traditional learning and many other topics. Ultimately, school districts should not invest in tablets for reading in the classroom because tablets prevent deep learning, promote distraction and the hefty upfront investment required is better spent on other programming.

Introduction and thesis statement

Traditional textbooks can be read in a more linear fashion that promotes deeper learning than studies show happens with tablet reading and learning. Several studies have proven that when watching people read on a computer or tablet, their eyes make an "E"-shaped movement and they end up seeing just about every other line, not every single line written, unlike with traditional texts where it's easier to read everything. More reading equates to more learning. Additionally, it's easier to pause and think with a traditional textbook, which often deepens the learning. Even though people pause reading on a tablet, it can be difficult to go back to the same exact point and eyes have a tendency to wander. Learning, thinking and reflecting happen more easily with a traditional textbook than with a tablet.

Supporting Paragraph: Example 1

In additional to being beneficial for learning, traditional textbooks do not require the same hefty upfront costs as a tablet and require virtually no maintenance beyond tape. Textbooks are much less expensive than tablets when buying a set for several hundred students in a particular school, and they need replacing much less often than tablets. And while the content is fixed in textbooks, with tablets there is always the chance of a breakdown, which leads to other consequences. Teachers who teach with tablets might have to become accustomed to hearing that a student couldn't do the required reading or research assignment because his or her tablet broke. Textbooks can be forgotten, and indeed often are, but they can also be easily retrieved, whereas it is not so easy to repair a tablet that is not working. The costs associated with tablets come with too large of a disadvantage when compared to traditional textbooks.

Supporting Paragraph: More examples

Beyond cost considerations, there are other issues with tablets. Though there is value in considering tablets for their ability to be updated and their low weight for student ease of carrying, ultimately students will learn better by using traditional textbooks. Distractions abound for students of every age and reading on a tablet only increases that distraction with the ability to do tasks beyond reading that come with the tablet format. The tablet is lightweight and easily updatable to be sure, but those physical advantages do not outweigh the cognitive disadvantages associated with tablet use.

Counter Argument with examples

When thinking through the comparison between tablets and traditional textbooks, several pros and cons must be measured, but ultimately given the considerations of cost and learning, the textbook is the better option for students.

Conclusion

NOTES

Made in the USA
Middletown, DE
06 September 2022

73292427R00126